And round and round the ring of them
Went dancing o'er the green

Memorial Edition

The Complete Works of
James Whitcomb Riley

IN TEN VOLUMES

*Including Poems and Prose Sketches, many
of which have not heretofore been published; an authentic Biography, an
elaborate Index and numerous
Illustrations from Paintings
by Howard Chandler Christy
and Ethel Franklin Betts*

VOLUME IV

*BOBBS-MERRILL
EDITION*

PUBLISHED BY

P. F. COLLIER & SON COMPANY

NEW YORK

CONTENTS

CONTENTS

CONTENTS

CONTENTS

The Complete Works
of James Whitcomb Riley

THE SOUTH WIND AND THE SUN

O THE South Wind and the Sun!
  How each loved the other one—
Full of fancy—full of folly—
  Full of jollity and fun!
  How they romped and ran about,
  Like two boys when school is out,
With glowing face, and lisping lip,
  Low laugh, and lifted shout!

  And the South Wind—he was dressed
  With a ribbon round his breast
That floated, flapped and fluttered
  In a riotous unrest,
  And a drapery of mist
  From the shoulder and the wrist
Flowing backward with the motion
  Of the waving hand he kissed.

And the Sun had on a crown
  Wrought of gilded thistle-down,
And a scarf of velvet vapor,
  And a raveled-rainbow gown;
  And his tinsel-tangled hair,
  Tossed and lost upon the air,
Was glossier and flossier
  Than any anywhere.

And the South Wind's eyes were two
  Little dancing drops of dew,
As he puffed his cheeks, and pursed his lips,
  And blew and blew and blew!
  And the Sun's—like diamond-stone,
  Brighter yet than ever known,
As he knit his brows and held his breath,
  And shone and shone and shone!

And this pair of merry fays
  Wandered through the summer days;
Arm in arm they went together
  Over heights of morning haze—
  Over slanting slopes of lawn
  Then went on and on and on,
Where the daisies looked like star-tracks
  Trailing up and down the dawn.

And where'er they found the top
  Of a wheat-stalk droop and lop
They chucked it underneath the chin
  And praised the lavish crop.

Till it lifted with the pride
Of the heads it grew beside,
And then the South Wind and the Sun
Went onward satisfied.

Over meadow-lands they tripped,
Where the dandelions dipped
In crimson foam of clover-bloom,
And dripped and dripped and dripped;
And they clinched the bumble-stings,
Gauming honey on their wings,
And bundling them in lily-bells,
With maudlin murmurings.

And the humming-bird, that hung
Like a jewel up among
The tilted honeysuckle-horns,
They mesmerized, and swung
In the palpitating air,
Drowsed with odors strange and rare,
And, with whispered laughter, slipped away,
And left him hanging there.

And they braided blades of grass
Where the truant had to pass;
And they wriggled through the rushes
And the reeds of the morass,
Where they danced, in rapture sweet,
O'er the leaves that laid a street
Of undulant mosaic for
The touches of their feet.

By the brook with mossy brink
　Where the cattle came to drink,
They trilled and piped and whistled
　With the thrush and bobolink,
　Till the kine, in listless pause,
　Switched their tails in mute applause,
With lifted heads, and dreamy eyes,
　And bubble-dripping jaws.

And where the melons grew,
　Streaked with yellow, green and blue,
These jolly sprites went wandering
　Through spangled paths of dew;
　And the melons, here and there,
　They made love to, everywhere,
Turning their pink souls to crimson
　With caresses fond and fair.

Over orchard walls they went,
　Where the fruited boughs were bent
Till they brushed the sward beneath them
　Where the shine and shadow blent;
　And the great green pear they shook
　Till the sallow hue forsook
Its features, and the gleam of gold
　Laughed out in every nook.

And they stroked the downy cheek
　Of the peach, and smoothed it sleek,
And flushed it into splendor;
　And, with many an elfish freak,

Gave the russet's rust a wipe—
Prankt the rambo with a stripe,
And the wine-sap blushed its reddest
As they spanked the pippins ripe.

Through the woven ambuscade
That the twining vines had made,
They found the grapes, in clusters,
Drinking up the shine and shade—
Plumpt, like tiny skins of wine,
With a vintage so divine
That the tongue of fancy tingled
With the tang of muscadine.

And the golden-banded bees,
Droning o'er the flowery leas,
They bridled, reined, and rode away
Across the fragrant breeze,
Till in hollow oak and elm
They had groomed and stabled them
In waxen stalls that oozed with dews
Of rose and lily-stem.

Where the dusty highway leads,
High above the wayside weeds,
They sowed the air with butterflies
Like blooming flower-seeds,
Till the dull grasshopper sprung
Half a man's height up, and hung
Tranced in the heat, with whirring wings,
And sung and sung and sung!

And they loitered, hand in hand,
  Where the snipe along the sand
Of the river ran to meet them
  As the ripple meets the land,
  Till the dragon-fly, in light
  Gauzy armor, burnished bright,
Came tilting down the waters
  In a wild, bewildered flight.

And they heard the killdee's call,
  And afar, the waterfall,
But the rustle of a falling leaf
  They heard above it all;
  And the trailing willow crept
  Deeper in the tide that swept
The leafy shallop to the shore,
  And wept and wept and wept!

And the fairy vessel veered
  From its moorings—tacked and steered
For the center of the current—
  Sailed away and disappeared:
  And the burthen that it bore
  From the long-enchanted shore—
"Alas! the South Wind and the Sun!"
  I murmur evermore.

For the South Wind and the Sun,
  Each so loves the other one,
For all his jolly folly
  And frivolity and fun,

That our love for them they weigh
As their fickle fancies may,
And when at last we love them most,
They laugh and sail away.

WHERE-AWAY

O THE Lands of Where-Away!
   Tell us—tell us—where are they?
Through the darkness and the dawn
We have journeyed on and on—
From the cradle to the cross—
From possession unto loss.—
Seeking still, from day to day,
For the Lands of Where-Away.

When our baby-feet were first
Planted where the daisies burst,
And the greenest grasses grew
In the fields we wandered through,—
On, with childish discontent,
Ever on and on we went,
Hoping still to pass, some day,
O'er the verge of Where-Away.

Roses laid their velvet lips
On our own, with fragrant sips;
But their kisses held us not,
All their sweetness we forgot;—

864

Though the brambles in our track
Plucked at us to hold us back—
"Just ahead," we used to say,
"Lie the Lands of Where-Away."

Children at the pasture-bars,
Through the dusk, like glimmering stars,
Waved their hands that we should bide
With them over eventide:
Down the dark their voices failed
Falteringly, as they hailed,
And died into yesterday—
Night ahead and—Where-Away?

Twining arms about us thrown—
Warm caresses, all our own,
Can but stay us for a spell—
Love hath little new to tell
To the soul in need supreme,
Aching ever with the dream
Of the endless bliss it may
Find in Lands of Where-Away!

THE SMITTEN PURIST

And the Charming Miss Smith's Effect Upon Him

THWEET Poethy! let me *lithp* forthwith,
 That I may thhing of the name of Smith—
   Which name, alath!
   In Harmony hath
No adequate rhyme, letht you grant me thith,—
That the thimple thibillant thound of *eth*—
(Which to thave my thoul, I can not expreth!)
   Thuth I may thhingingly,
   Wooingly and winningly
   Thu—thu—thound in the name of Smith.

O give me a name that will rhyme with Smith,—
For wild and weird ath the sthrange name ith,
   I would sthrangle a sthrain
   And a thad refrain
Faint and sthweet ath a whithpered kissth;
I would thhing thome thong for the mythtic
 mitth
Who beareth the thingular name of Smith—
   The dathzlingly brilli-ant,
   Rarely rethilliant
   Ap—pup—pellation of Smith!

O had I a name that would rhyme with Smith—
Thome rhythmical tincture of rethonant blith—
      Thome melody rare
      Ath the cherubth blare
On them little trumpeths they're foolin' with—
I would thit me down, and I'd thhing like thith
Of the girl of the thingular name of Smith—
      The sthrangely curiouth,
      Rich and luxuriouth
     Pup—patronymic of Smith!

CHRISTINE BRAIBRY

THE BEAUTIFUL DOLLY WHO COMES FROM
TENTOLEENA LAND
BRINGING A STRANGE LETTER

The Letter

THIS little Dolly's name is Christine Braibry.*
She was born in Tentoleena Land, where lilies
and red roses grow in the air, and humming-birds
and butterflies on stalks.

You must be kind to Christine, for everything
about her in your land will be very strange to her.
If she seems to stare in a bewildered way, and will
not answer when you ask her why, you must know
that she is simply dazed with the wonders that she
sees on every hand. It will doubtless be a long, long
while before Christine will cease to marvel at the
Sunshine of your strange country; for in Tentoleena Land there is never any shine but Moonshine,
and sometimes that gets so muddied up with shade
it soils the eyesight to gaze at it overmuch.

It will be trying, in your land, for Christine to
keep silent all the time, for, in your country, Dollies

---

*The terminal of this name is sounded short, as in "lovely."

868

can not walk and talk at all perfectly, because they only think they are dreaming all the time, and they dare not speak for fear their voices will awaken them, and they dare not move for fear of falling out of bed. So, you see, you should be very kind indeed to little Christine Braibry.

In Tentoleena Land the Dollies do not sleep long —they are always the first ones up at Moon-dawn— for Moon-dawn is the Dollies' morning. Then they go out in the fragrant grasses, where the big, ripe dewdrops grow—much nicer, purer dew than yours on earth, for in Tentoleena Land they gather it before it has been skimmed, and all the pearly cream that gathers on the surface of the drops they stir up with the rest and bathe in that; and this is why the Dollies always have such delicate complexions. Then, when the baths are over, they dress themselves, and waken their parents, and dress them— for in Tentoleena Land the parents are the children. Is not that odd?

Sometime Christine may get used to your strange land and all the wonders that she sees; and if she ever does, and smiles at you, and pulls your face down close to hers and kisses you, why, that will be the sign by which you'll know she's coming to again and wants to talk; and so the first thing you must ask of her is to sing this little song she made of Tentoleena Land. Only the words of it can be given here—(not half the beauty of the dainty song)—for when you *hear* it, in the marvelously faint, and low, and sweet, and tender, tinkling

tongue of Tentoleena Land, you will indeed be glad
that the gracious fairy Fortune ever sent you
Christine Braibry.

So, since all the sounds in the melodious utter-
ance of Tentoleena Land are so exquisitely, so
chastely, rarely beautiful no earthly art may hope to
reproduce them, you must, as you here read the
words, just shut your eyes and *fancy* that you hear
little Christine Braibry singing this eery song of
hers:—

CHRISTINE'S SONG

UP in Tentoleena Land—
    Tentoleena! Tentoleena!
All the Dollies, hand in hand,
    Mina, Nainie, and Serena,
Dance the Fairy fancy dances,
With glad songs and starry glances,
Lisping roundelays; and, after,
Bird-like interludes of laughter
Strewn and scattered o'er the lawn
Their gilt sandals twinkle on
Through light mists of silver sand—
    Up in Tentoleena Land.

Up in Tentoleena Land—
    Tentoleena! Tentoleena!
Blares the eery Elfin band—
    Trumpet, harp and concertina—

Larkspur bugle—honeysuckle
Cornet, with a quickstep chuckle
In its golden throat; and, maybe,
Lilies-of-the-valley they be
Baby-silver-bells that chime
Musically all the time,
Tossed about from hand to hand—
     Up in Tentoleena Land.

Up in Tentoleena Land—
     Tentoleena! Tentoleena!
Dollies dark, and blond and bland—
     Sweet as musk-rose or verbena—
Sweet as moon-blown daffodillies,
Or wave-jostled water-lilies
Yearning to'rd the rose-mouths, ready
Leaning o'er the river's eddy,—
Dance, and glancing fling to you,
Through these lines you listen to,
Kisses blown from lip and hand
     Out of Tentoleena Land!

DEAR HANDS

THE touches of her hands are like the fall
  Of velvet snowflakes; like the touch of down
The peach just brushes 'gainst the garden wall;
The flossy fondlings of the thistle-wisp
  Caught in the crinkle of a leaf of brown
The blighting frost hath turned from green to crisp

Soft as the falling of the dusk at night,
The touches of her hands, and the delight—
  The touches of her hands!
The touches of her hands are like the dew
That falls so softly down no one e'er knew
The touch thereof save lovers like to one
Astray in lights where ranged Endymion.

O rarely soft, the touches of her hands,
As drowsy zephyrs in enchanted lands;
  Or pulse of dying fay; or fairy sighs;
Or—in between the midnight and the dawn,
When long unrest and tears and fears are gone—
  Sleep, smoothing down the lids of weary eyes.

872

WINTER FANCIES

I

WINTER without
　　And warmth within;
The winds may shout
　　And the storm begin;
The snows may pack
　　At the window-pane,
And the skies grow black,
　　And the sun remain
Hidden away
　　The livelong day—
But here—in here is the warmth of May!

II

Swoop your spitefulest
　　Up the flue,
　　Wild Winds—do!
What in the world do I care for you?
　　O delightfulest
　　Weather of all,
　　Howl and squall,
And shake the trees till the last leaves fall!

III

The joy one feels,
　　In an easy-chair,
Cocking his heels
　　In the dancing air
That wreathes the rim of a roaring stove
Whose heat loves better than hearts can love,
　　Will not permit
　　　　The coldest day
　　　　　　To drive away
The fire in his blood, and the bliss of it!

IV

Then blow, Winds, blow!
　　And rave and shriek,
And snarl and snow,
　　Till your breath grows weak—
While here in my room
　　I'm as snugly shut
As a glad little worm
　　In the heart of a nut!

"A BRAVE REFRAIN"

WHEN snow is here, and the trees look weird,
  And the knuckled twigs are gloved with
    frost;
When the breath congeals in the drover's beard,
  And the old pathway to the barn is lost;
When the rooster's crow is sad to hear,
  And the stamp of the stabled horse is vain,
And the tone of the cow-bell grieves the ear—
  O then is the time for a brave refrain!

When the gears hang stiff on the harness-peg,
  And the tallow gleams in frozen streaks;
And the old hen stands on a lonesome leg,
  And the pump sounds hoarse and the handle
    squeaks;
When the wood-pile lies in a shrouded heap,
  And the frost is scratched from the window-pane
And anxious eyes from the inside peep—
  O then is the time for a brave refrain!

When the ax-helve warms at the chimney-jamb,
  And hobnailed shoes on the hearth below,
And the house-cat curls in a slumber calm,
  And the eight-day clock ticks loud and slow;

When the harsh broom-handle jabs the ceil
　'Neath the kitchen-loft, and the drowsy brain
Sniffs the breath of the morning meal—
　O then is the time for a brave refrain!

Envoi

When the skillet seethes, and a blubbering hot
Tilts the lid of the coffee-pot,
And the scent of the buckwheat cake grows plain—
O then is the time for a brave refrain!

AS I SIT IN THE SILENCE

M ANY pleasures of Youth have been buoyantly
　　sung—
　And, borne on the winds of delight, may they
　　　beat
With their palpitant wings at the hearts of the
　　　Young,
　And in bosoms of Age find as warm a retreat!—
Yet sweetest of all of the musical throng,
　Though least of the numbers that upward aspire,
Is the one rising now into wavering song,
　As I sit in the silence and gaze in the fire.

'Tis a Winter long dead that beleaguers my door
　And muffles his steps in the snows of the past:
And I see, in the embers I'm dreaming before,
　Lost faces of love as they looked on me last:—
The round, laughing eyes of the desk-mate of old
　Gleam out for a moment with truant desire—
Then fade and are lost in a City of Gold,
　As I sit in the silence and gaze in the fire.

And then comes the face, peering back in my own,
  Of a shy little girl, with her lids drooping low,
As she faltering tells, in a far-away tone,
  The ghost of a story of long, long ago.—
Then her dewy blue eyes they are lifted again;
  But I see their glad light slowly fail and expire,
As I reach and cry to her in vain, all in vain!—
  As I sit in the silence and gaze in the fire.

Then the face of a Mother looks back, through the
      mist
  Of the tears that are welling; and, lucent with
      light,
I see the dear smile of the lips I have kissed
  As she knelt by my cradle at morning and night;
And my arms are outheld, with a yearning too wild
  For any but God in His love to inspire,
As she pleads at the foot of His throne for her
      child,—
  As I sit in the silence and gaze in the fire.

O pathos of rapture! O glorious pain!
  My heart is a blossom of joy overrun
With a shower of tears, as a lily with rain
  That weeps in the shadow and laughs in the sun.
The blight of the frost may descend on the tree,
  And the leaf and the flower may fall and expire,
But ever and ever love blossoms for me,
  As I sit in the silence and gaze in the fire.

"As I sit in the silence"

LONGFELLOW'S LOVE FOR THE CHILDREN

AWAKE, he loved their voices,
  And wove them into his rhyme;
And the music of their laughter
  Was with him all the time.

Though he knew the tongues of nations,
  And their meanings all were dear,
The prattle and lisp of a little child
  Was the sweetest for him to hear.

A SONG OF LONG AGO

A SONG of Long Ago:
  Sing it lightly—sing it low—
Sing it softly—like the lisping of the lips
    we used to know
When our baby-laughter spilled
From the glad hearts ever filled
With music blithe as robin ever trilled!

Let the fragrant summer breeze,
And the leaves of locust-trees,
And the apple-buds and -blossoms, and the
    wings of honey-bees,
All palpitate with glee,
Till the happy harmony
Brings back each childish joy to you and me.

Let the eyes of fancy turn
Where the tumbled pippins burn
Like embers in the orchard's lap of tangled
    grass and fern,—
There let the old path wind
In and out, and on behind
The cider-press that chuckles as we grind.

Blend in the song the moan
Of the dove that grieves alone,
And the wild whir of the locust, and the
    bumble's drowsy drone;
And the low of cows that call
Through the pasture-bars when all
The landscape fades away at evenfall.

Then, far away and clear,
Through the dusky atmosphere,
Let the wailing of the killdee be the only
    sound we hear:
O sad and sweet and low
As the memory may know
Is the glad-pathetic song of Long Ago!

UNLESS

WHO has not *wanted* does not guess
    What plenty is.—Who has not groped
In depths of doubt and hopelessness
    Has never truly hoped.—
Unless, sometimes, a shadow falls
    Upon his mirth, and veils his sight,
    And from the darkness drifts the light
Of love at intervals.

And that most dear of everything,
    I hold, is love; and who can sit
With lightest heart and laugh and sing,
    Knows not the worth of it.—
Unless, in some strange throng, perchance,
    He feels how thrilling sweet it is,
    One yearning look that answers his—
The troth of glance and glance.

Who knows not pain, knows not, alas!
    What pleasure is.—Who knows not of
The bitter cup that will not pass,
    Knows not the taste of love.

882

O souls that thirst, and hearts that fast,
　And natures faint with famishing,
　God lift and lead and safely bring
You to your own at last!

WHEN EARLY MARCH SEEMS MIDDLE MAY

WHEN country roads begin to thaw
    In mottled spots of damp and dust,
And fences by the margin draw
    Along the frosty crust
Their graphic silhouettes, I say,
The Spring is coming round this way.

When morning-time is bright with sun
    And keen with wind, and both confuse
The dancing, glancing eyes of one
    With tears that ooze and ooze—
And nose-tips weep as well as they,
The Spring is coming round this way.

When suddenly some shadow-bird
    Goes wavering beneath the gaze,
And through the hedge the moan is heard
    Of kine that fain would graze
In grasses new, I smile and say,
The Spring is coming round this way.

When knotted horse-tails are untied,
    And teamsters whistle here and there,
And clumsy mitts are laid aside
    And choppers' hands are bare,
And chips are thick where children play,
The Spring is coming round this way.

When through the twigs the farmer tramps,
    And troughs are chunked beneath the trees,
And fragrant hints of sugar-camps
    Astray in every breeze,—
When early March seems middle May,
The Spring is coming round this way.

When coughs are changed to laughs, and when
    Our frowns melt into smiles of glee,
And all our blood thaws out again
    In streams of ecstasy,
And poets wreak their roundelay,
The Spring is coming round this way.

THE MUSKINGUM VALLEY

THE Muskingum Valley!—How longin' the
  gaze
A feller throws back on its long summer days,
When the smiles of its blossoms and *my* smiles wuz
  one-
And-the-same, from the rise to the set o' the sun:
Wher' the hills sloped as soft as the dawn down to
  noon,
And the river run by like an old fiddle-tune,
And the hours glided past as the bubbles 'ud glide,
All so loaferin'-like, 'long the path o' the tide.

In the Muskingum Valley—it 'peared like the skies
Looked lovin' on me as my own mother's eyes,
While the laughin'-sad song of the stream seemed
  to be
Like a lullaby angels was wastin' on me—
Tel, swimmin' the air, like the gossamer's thread,
'Twixt the blue underneath and the blue overhead,
My thoughts went astray in that so-to-speak realm
Wher' Sleep bared her breast as a piller fer them.

In the Muskingum Valley, though far, far a-way,
I know that the winter is bleak there to-day—
No bloom ner perfume on the brambles er trees—
Wher' the buds ust to bloom, now the icicles
 freeze.—
That the grass is all hid 'long the side of the road
Wher' the deep snow has drifted and shifted and
 blowed—
And I feel in my life the same changes is there,—
The frost in my heart, and the snow in my hair.

But, Muskingum Valley! my memory sees
Not the white on the ground, but the green in the
 trees—
Not the froze'-over gorge, but the current, as clear
And warm as the drop that has jes' trickled here;
Not the choked-up ravine, and the hills topped with
 snow,
But the grass and the blossoms I knowed long ago
When my little bare feet wundered down wher' the
 stream
In the Muskingum Valley flowed on like a dream.

SERENADE—TO NORA

THE moonlight is failin'—
   The sad stars are palin'—
The black wings av night are a-dhroopin' an'
            trailin';
      The wind's miserere
      Sounds lonesome an' dreary;
The katydid's dumb an' the nightingale's weary.

      Troth, Nora! I'm wadin'
      The grass an' paradin'
The dews at your dure, wid my swate serenadin',
      Alone and forsaken,
      Whilst you're never wakin'
To tell me you're wid me an' I am mistaken!

      Don't think that my singin'
      It's wrong to be flingin'
Forninst av the dreams that the Angels are bringin';
      For if your pure spirit
      Might waken and hear it,
You'd never be draamin' the Saints could come
            near it!

Then lave off your slaapin'—
The pulse av me's laapin'
To have the two eyes av yez down on me paapin'.
Och, Nora! It's hopin'
Your windy ye'll open
And light up the night where the heart av me's
gropin'.

THE LITTLE WHITE HEARSE

AS the little white hearse went glimmering by—
The man on the coal-cart jerked his lines,
And smutted the lid of either eye,
And turned and stared at the business signs;
And the street-car driver stopped and beat
His hands on his shoulders, and gazed up-street
Till his eye on the long track reached the sky—
As the little white hearse went glimmering by.

As the little white hearse went glimmering by—
A stranger petted a ragged child
In the crowded walks, and she knew not why,
But he gave her a coin for the way she smiled;
And a boot-black thrilled with a pleasure
strange
As a customer put back his change
With a kindly hand and a grateful sigh,
As the little white hearse went glimmering by.

As the little white hearse went glimmering by—
A man looked out of a window dim,
And his cheeks were wet and his heart was dry,
For a dead child even was dear to him!
And he thought of his empty life, and said:—
"Loveless alive, and loveless dead—
Nor wife nor child in earth or sky!"
As the little white hearse went glimmering by.

A GLIMPSE OF PAN

I CAUGHT but a glimpse of him.   Summer was
here,
And I strayed from the town and its dust and
heat,
And walked in a wood, while the noon was near,
Where the shadows were cool, and the atmosphere
Was misty with fragrances stirred by my feet
From surges of blossoms that billowed sheer
Of the grasses, green and sweet.

And I peered through a vista of leaning trees,
Tressed with long tangles of vines that swept
To the face of a river, that answered these
With vines in the wave like the vines in the breeze,
Till the yearning lips of the ripples crept
And kissed them, with quavering ecstasies,
And wistfully laughed and wept.

And there, like a dream in a swoon, I swear
I saw Pan lying,—his limbs in the dew
And the shade, and his face in the dazzle and glare
Of the glad sunshine; while everywhere,
Over, across, and around him blew
Filmy dragon-flies hither and there,
And little white butterflies, two and two,
In eddies of odorous air.

THE GREAT GOD PAN

What was he doing, the great god Pan!
—MRS. BROWNING

O PAN is the goodliest god, I wist,
  Of all of the lovable gods that be!—
For his two strong hands were the first to twist
From the depths of the current, through spatter
    and mist,
  The long-hushed reeds that he pressed in glee
To his murmurous mouth, as he chuckled and kissed
  Their souls into melody.

And the wanton winds are in love with Pan:
  They loll in the shade with him day by day;
And betimes as beast, and betimes as man,
They love him as only the wild winds can,—
  Or sleeking the coat of his limbs one way,
Or brushing his brow with the locks they fan
  To the airs he loves to play.

And he leans by the river, in gloom and gleam,
  Blowing his reeds as the breezes blow—
His cheeks puffed out, and his eyes in a dream,

And his hoof-tips, over the leaves in the stream,
  Tapping the time of the tunes that flow
As sweet as the drowning echoes seem
  To his rollicking wraith below.

HER LIGHT GUITAR

SHE twankled a tune on her light guitar—
    A low, sweet jangle of tangled sounds,
As blurred as the voices of the fairies are,
    Dancing in moondawn dales and downs;
        And the tinkling drip of the strange refrain
        Ran over the rim of my soul like rain.

The great blond moon in the midnight skies
    Paused and poised o'er the trellis eaves,
And the stars, in the light of her upturned eyes,
    Sifted their love through the rifted leaves—
        Glittered and splintered in crystal mist
        Down the glittering strings that her fingers
            kissed.

O the melody mad! O the tinkle and thrill
    Of the ecstasy of the exquisite thing!
The red rose dropped from the window-sill
    And lay in a long swoon quivering;
        While the dying notes of the strain divine
        Rippled in glee up my spell-bound spine.

THE ALL-GOLDEN

I

THROUGH every happy line I sing
I feel the tonic of the Spring.
The day is like an old-time face
That gleams across some grassy place—
An old-time face—an old-time chum
Who rises from the grave to come
And lure me back along the ways
Of time's all-golden yesterdays.
Sweet day! to thus remind me of
The truant boy I used to love—
To set, once more, his finger-tips
Against the blossom of his lips,
And pipe for me the signal known
By none but him and me alone!

II

I see, across the schoolroom floor,
The shadow of the open door,
And dancing dust and sunshine blent
Slanting the way the morning went,

And beckoning my thoughts afar
Where reeds and running waters are;
Where amber-colored bayous glass
The half-drown'd weeds and wisps of grass,
Where sprawling frogs, in loveless key,
Sing on and on incessantly.
Against the green wood's dim expanse
The cattail tilts its tufted lance,
While on its tip—one might declare
The white "snake-feeder" blossomed there!

III

I catch my breath, as children do
In woodland swings when life is new,
And all the blood is warm as wine
And tingles with a tang divine.
My soul soars up the atmosphere
And sings aloud where God can hear,
And all my being leans intent
To mark His smiling wonderment.
O gracious dream, and gracious time,
And gracious theme, and gracious rhyme—
When buds of Spring begin to blow
In blossoms that we used to know
And lure us back along the ways
Of time's all-golden yesterdays!

THE WAY THE BABY CAME

O THIS is the way the baby came:
　　Out of the night as comes the dawn
Out of the embers as the flame;
　Out of the bud the blossom on
The apple-bough that blooms the same
　As in glad summers dead and gone—
With a grace and beauty none could name—
O this is the way the baby came!

THE WAY THE BABY WOKE

AND this is the way the baby woke:
  As when in deepest drops of dew
The shine and shadows sink and soak,
  The sweet eyes glimmered through and
      through;
And eddyings and dimples broke
  About the lips, and no one knew
Or could divine the words they spoke—
And this is the way the baby woke.

THE WAY THE BABY SLEPT

THIS is the way the baby slept:
   A mist of tresses backward thrown
By quavering sighs where kisses crept
   With yearnings she had never known:
The little hands were closely kept
   About a lily newly blown—
And God was with her. And we wept.—
And this is the way the baby slept.

WHEN MAIMIE MARRIED

WHEN Maimie married Charley Brown,
    Joy took possession of the town;
The young folks swarmed in happy throngs—
They rang the bells—they caroled songs—
They carpeted the steps that led
Into the church where they were wed;
And up and down the altar-stair
They scattered roses everywhere;
When, in her orange-blossom crown,
Queen Maimie married Charley Brown.

So beautiful she was, it seemed
Men, looking on her, dreamed they dreamed;
And he, the holy man who took
Her hand in his, so thrilled and shook,
The gargoyles round the ceiling's rim
Looked down and leered and grinned at him,
Until he half forgot his part
Of sanctity, and felt his heart
Beat worldward through his sacred gown—
When Maimie married Charley Brown.

The bridesmaids kissed her, left and right—
Fond mothers hugged her with delight—
Young men of twenty-seven were seen
To blush like lads of seventeen,
The while they held her hand to quote
Such sentiments as poets wrote.—
Yea, all the heads that Homage bends
Where bowed to her.—But O my friends,
My hopes went up—*my* heart went down—
When Maimie married—*Charley Brown!*

HER HAIR

THE beauty of her hair bewilders me—
　　Pouring adown the brow, its cloven tide
　Swirling about the ears on either side
And storming round the neck tumultuously:
Or like the lights of old antiquity
　Through mullioned windows, in cathedrals wide,
　Spilled moltenly o'er figures deified
In chastest marble, nude of drapery.
And so I love it.—Either unconfined;
　Or plaited in close braidings manifold;
Or smoothly drawn; or indolently twined
　In careless knots whose coilings come unrolled
At any lightest kiss; or by the wind
　Whipped out in flossy ravelings of gold.

A VISION OF SUMMER

'TWAS a marvelous vision of Summer.—
    That morning the dawn was late,
And came, like a long dream-ridden guest,
    Through the gold of the Eastern gate.

Languid it came, and halting
    As one that yawned, half roused,
With lifted arms and indolent lids
    And eyes that drowsed and drowsed.

A glimmering haze hung over
    The face of the smiling air;
And the green of the trees and the blue of
    the leas
And the skies gleamed everywhere.

And the dewdrops' dazzling jewels,
    In garlands and diadems,
Lightened and twinkled and glanced and shot
    At the glints of a thousand gems:

Emeralds of dew on the grasses;
    The rose with rubies set;
On the lily, diamonds; and amethysts
    Pale on the violet.

And there were the pinks of the fuchsias,
    And the peony's crimson hue,
The lavender of the hollyhocks,
    And the morning-glory's blue:

The purple of the pansy bloom,
    And the passionate flush of the face
Of the velvet-rose; and the thick perfume
    Of the locust every place.

The air and the sun and the shadows
    Were wedded and made as one;
And the winds ran over the meadows
    As little children run:

And the winds poured over the meadows
    And along the willowy way
The river ran, with its ripples shod
    With the sunshine of the day:

O the winds flowed over the meadows
    In a tide of eddies and calms,
And the bared brow felt the touch of it
    As a sweetheart's tender palms.

And the lark went palpitating
  Up through the glorious skies,
His song spilled down from the blue profound
  As a song from Paradise.

And here was the loitering current—
  Stayed by a drift of sedge
And sodden logs—scummed thick with the
    gold
  Of the pollen from edge to edge.

The catbird piped in the hazel,
  And the harsh kingfisher screamed;
And the crane, in amber and oozy swirls,
  Dozed in the reeds and dreamed.

And in through the tumbled driftage
  And the tangled roots below,
The waters warbled and gurgled and lisped
  Like the lips of long ago.

And the senses caught, through the music,
  Twinkles of dabbling feet,
And glimpses of faces in coverts green,
  And voices faint and sweet.

And back from the lands enchanted,
  Where my earliest mirth was born,
The trill of a laugh was blown to me
  Like the blare of an elfin horn.

Again I romped through the clover;
   And again I lay supine
On grassy swards, where the skies, like eyes,
   Looked lovingly back to mine.

And over my vision floated
   Misty illusive things—
Trailing strands of the gossamer
   On heavenward wanderings:

Figures that veered and wavered,
   Luring the sight, and then
Glancing away into nothingness,
   And blinked into shape again.

From out far depths of the forest,
   Ineffably sad and lorn,
Like the yearning cry of a long-lost love,
   The moan of the dove was borne.

And through lush glooms of the thicket
   The flash of the redbird's wings
On branches of star-white blooms that shook
   And thrilled with its twitterings.

Through mossy and viny vistas,
   Soaked ever with deepest shade,
Dimly the dull owl stared and stared
   From his bosky ambuscade.

And up through the rifted tree-tops
   That signaled the wayward breeze,
I saw the hulk of the hawk becalmed
   Far out on the azure seas.

Then sudden an awe fell on me,
   As the hush of the golden day
Rounded to noon, as a May to June
   That a lover has dreamed away.

And I heard, in the breathless silence,
   And the full, glad light of the sun,
The tinkle and drip of a timorous shower—
   Ceasing as it begun.

And my thoughts, like the leaves and grasses,
   In a rapture of joy and pain,
Seemed fondled and petted and beat upon
   With a tremulous patter of rain.

WHILE CIGARETTES TO ASHES TURN

I

"HE smokes—and that's enough," says
      Ma—
"And cigarettes, at that!" says Pa.

"He must not call again," says she—
"He *shall* not call again!" says he.

They both glare at me as before—
Then quit the room and bang the door,—

While I, their wilful daughter, say,
"I guess I'll love him, anyway!"

II

At twilight, in his room, alone,
His careless feet inertly thrown

Across a chair, my fancy can
But worship this most worthless man!

I dream what joy it is to set
His slow lips round a cigarette,

With idle-humored whiff and puff—
Ah! this is innocent enough!

To mark the slender fingers raise
The waxen match's dainty blaze,

Whose chastened light an instant glows
On drooping lids and arching nose,

Then, in the sudden gloom, instead,
A tiny ember, dim and red,

Blooms languidly to ripeness, then
Fades slowly, and grows ripe again.

III

I lean back, in my own boudoir—
The door is fast, the sash ajar;

And in the dark, I smiling stare
At one wide window over there,

Where some one, smoking, pinks the gloom,
The darling darkness of his room!

I push my shutters wider yet,
And lo! I light a cigarette;

And gleam for gleam, and glow for glow,
Each pulse of light a word we know,

We talk of love that still will burn
While cigarettes to ashes turn.

THE LITTLE RED RIBBON

THE little red ribbon, the ring and the rose!
The summer-time comes, and the summer-
time goes—
And never a blossom in all of the land
As white as the gleam of her beckoning hand!

The long winter months, and the glare of the snows;
The little red ribbon, the ring and the rose!
And never a glimmer of sun in the skies
As bright as the light of her glorious eyes!

Dreams only are true; but they fade and are gone—
For her face is not here when I waken at dawn;
The little red ribbon, the ring and the rose
Mine only; *hers* only the dream and repose.

I am weary of waiting, and weary of tears,
And my heart wearies, too, all these desolate years,
Moaning over the one only song that it knows,—
The little red ribbon, the ring and the rose!

THE MAN IN THE MOON

SAID The Raggedy Man, on a hot afternoon:
 My!
  Sakes!
   What a lot o' mistakes
Some little folks makes on The Man in the Moon!
But people that's be'n up to *see* him, like *me,*
And calls on him frequent and intimuttly,
Might drop a few facts that would interest you
  Clean!
   Through!—
    If you wanted 'em to—
Some *actual* facts that might interest you!

O The Man in the Moon has a crick in his back;
  Whee!
   Whimm!
    Ain't you sorry for him?
And a mole on his nose that is purple and black;
And his eyes are so weak that they water and run
If he dares to *dream* even he looks at the sun,—

So he jes' dreams of stars, as the doctors advise—
  My!
    Eyes!
        But isn't he wise—
To jes' dream of stars, as the doctors advise?

And The Man in the Moon has a boil on his ear—
  Whee!
    Whing!
        What a singular thing!
I know! but these facts are authentic, my dear,—
There's a boil on his ear; and a corn on his chin—
He calls it a dimple—but dimples stick in—
Yet it might be a dimple turned over, you know!
  Whang!
    Ho!
        Why, certainly so!—
It might be a dimple turned over, you know!

And The Man in the Moon has a rheumatic
        knee—
  Gee!
    Whizz!
        What a pity that is!
And his toes have worked round where his heels
        ought to be.—
So whenever he wants to go North he goes *South,*
And comes back with porridge-crumbs all round
        his mouth,

And he brushes them off with a Japanese fan,
  Whing!
    Whann!
      What a marvelous man!
What a very remarkably marvelous man!

And The Man in the Moon, sighed The Raggedy
      Man,
  Gits!
    So!
        Sullonesome, you know,—
Up there by hisse'f sence creation began!—
That when I call on him and then come away,
He grabs me and holds me and begs me to stay,—
Till—*Well!* if it wasn't fer *Jimmy-cum-jim,*
  Dadd!
    Limb!
        I'd go pardners with him—
Jes' jump my job here and be pardners with
    him!

A BAREFOOT BOY

A BAREFOOT boy! I mark him at his play--
  For May is here once more, and so is he,—
His dusty trousers, rolled half to the knee,
And his bare ankles grimy, too, as they:
Cross-hatchings of the nettle, in array
  Of feverish stripes, hint vividly to me
  Of woody pathways winding endlessly
Along the creek, where even yesterday

He plunged his shrinking body—gasped and shook—
  Yet called the water "warm," with never lack
Of joy.   And so, half enviously I look
  Upon this graceless barefoot and his track,—
  His toe stubbed—ay, his big toe-nail knocked back
Like unto the clasp of an old pocketbook.

"THE PREACHER'S BOY"

I RICKOLLECT the little tad, back, years and
 years ago—
"The Preacher's Boy" that every one despised and
 hated so!
A meek-faced little feller, with white eyes and foxy
 hair,
And a look like he expected ser'ous trouble everywhere:
A sort o' fixed expression of suspicion in his glance;
His bare feet always scratched with briers; and
 green stains on his pants;
Molasses-marks along his sleeves; his cap-rim
 turned behind—
And so it is "The Preacher's Boy" is brought again
 to mind!

My fancy even brings the sly marauder back so
 plain,
I see him jump our garden-fence and slip off down
 the lane;
And I seem to holler at him and git back the old
 reply:
"Oh, no: your peaches is too green fer such a worm
 as I!"

916

Fer he scorned his father's phrases—every holy one
    he had—
"As good a man," folks put it, "as that boy of his
    was bad!"
And again from their old buggy-shed, I hear the
    "rod unspared"—
Of course that never "spoiled the child" for which
    nobody cared!

If any neighber ever found his gate without a latch,
Or rines around the edges of his watermelon-patch;
His pasture-bars left open; or his pump-spout
    chocked with clay,
He'd swear 'twas "that infernal Preacher's Boy,"
    right away!
When strings was stretched acrost the street at
    night, and some one got
An everlastin' tumble, and his nose broke, like as
    not,
And laid it on "The Preacher's Boy"—no powers,
    low ner high,
Could ever quite substantiate that boy's alibi!

And did *nobody* like the boy?—Well, all the *pets* in
    town
Would eat out of his fingers; and canaries would
    come down
And leave their swingin' perches and their fish-bone
    jist to pick
The little warty knuckles that the dogs would leap
    to lick.—

No little snarlin', snappin' fiste but what would leave
    his bone
To foller, ef *he* whistled, in that tantalizin' tone
That made a goods-box whittler blasphemeusly
    protest
"He couldn't tell, 'twixt dog and boy, which one
    was ornriest!"

'Twas such a little cur as this, onc't, when the crowd
    was thick
Along the streets, a drunken corner-loafer tried to
    kick,
When a sudden foot behind him tripped him up, and
    falling so
He "marked his man," and jerked his gun—drawed
    up and let 'er go!
And the crowd swarmed round the victim—holding
    close against his breast
The little dog unharmed, in arms that still, as they
    caressed,
Grew rigid in their last embrace, as with a smile of
    joy
He recognized the dog was saved. So died "The
    Preacher's Boy"!

When it appeared, before the Squire, that fatal
    pistol-ball
Was fired at "a dangerous beast," and not the boy at
    all,

And the facts set forth established,—it was like-
befittin' then

To order out a possy of the "city councilmen"

To kill *the dog!* But, strange to tell, they searched
the country round,

And never hide-ner-hair of that "said" dog was ever
found!

And, somehow, *then* I sort o' thought—and half-
way think, *to-day*—

The spirit of "The Preacher's Boy" had whistled
him away.

WE TO SIGH INSTEAD OF SING

"RAIN and rain! and rain and rain!"
    Yesterday we muttered
Grimly as the grim refrain
    That the thunders uttered:
All the heavens under cloud—
    All the sunshine sleeping;
All the grasses limply bowed
    With their weight of weeping.

Sigh and sigh! and sigh and sigh!
    Never end of sighing;
Rain and rain for our reply—
    Hopes half drowned and dying;
Peering through the window-pane,
    Naught but endless raining—
Endless sighing, and, as vain,
    Endlessly complaining.

Shine and shine! and shine and shine!
    Ah! to-day the splendor!—
All this glory yours and mine—
    God! but God is tender!

We to sigh instead of sing,
Yesterday, in sorrow,
While the Lord was fashioning
This for our To-morrow!

NOTHIN' TO SAY

NOTHIN' to say, my daughter! Nothin' at all
    to say!
Gyrls that's in love, I've noticed, giner'ly has their
    way!
Yer mother did, afore you, when her folks objected
    to me—
Yit here I am and here you air! and yer mother—
    where is she?

You look lots like yer mother: purty much same in
    size;
And about the same complected; and favor about
    the eyes:
Like her, too, about livin' here, because *she* couldn't
    stay;
It'll 'most seem like you was dead like her!—but I
    hain't got nothin' to say!

She left you her little Bible—writ yer name acrost
    the page—
And left her ear-bobs fer you, ef ever you come of
    age;
I've alluz kep' 'em and gyuarded 'em, but ef yer
    goin' away—
Nothin' to say, my daughter! Nothin' at all to say!

You don't rickollect her, I reckon? No: you wasn't
     a year old then!
And now yer—how old *air* you? W'y, child, not
     "twenty"! When?
And yer nex' birthday's in Aprile? and you want to
     git married that day?
I wisht yer mother was livin'!—but I hain't got
     nothin' to say!

Twenty year! and as good a gyrl as parent ever
     found!
There's a straw ketched on to yer dress there—I'll
     bresh it off—turn round.
(Her mother was jes' twenty when us two run
     away.)
Nothin' to say, my daughter! Nothin' at all to say!

JACK-IN-THE-BOX

Grandfather, musing

IN childish days! O memory,
  You bring such curious things to me!—
Laughs to the lip—tears to the eye,
In looking on the gifts that lie
Like broken playthings scattered o'er
Imagination's nursery floor!
Did these old hands once click the key
That let "Jack's" box-lid upward fly,
And that blear-eyed, fur-whiskered elf
Leap, as though frightened at himself,
And quiveringly lean and stare
At me, his jailer, laughing there?

A child then! Now—I only know
They call me very old; and so
They will not let me have my way,—
But uselessly I sit all day
Here by the chimney-jamb, and poke
The lazy fire, and smoke and smoke,

And watch the wreaths swoop up the flue,
And chuckle—ay, I often do—
Seeing again, all vividly,
Jack-in-the-box leap, as in glee
To see how much he looks like me!

. . . . They talk. I can't hear what they
    say—
But I am glad, clean through and through
Sometimes, in fancying that they
Are saying, "Sweet, that fancy strays
In age back to our childish days!"

THE OLD TRUNDLE-BED

O THE old trundle-bed where I slept when a
     boy!
What canopied king might not covet the joy?
The glory and peace of that slumber of mine,
Like a long, gracious rest in the bosom divine:
The quaint, homely couch, hidden close from the
     light,
But daintily drawn from its hiding at night.
O a nest of delight, from the foot to the head,
Was the queer little, dear little, old trundle-bed!

O the old trundle-bed, where I wondering saw
The stars through the window, and listened with
     awe
To the sigh of the winds as they tremblingly crept
Through the trees where the robin so restlessly
     slept:
Where I heard the low, murmurous chirp of the
     wren,
And the katydid listlessly chirrup again,
Till my fancies grew faint and were drowsily led
Through the maze of the dreams of the old trundle-
     bed.

O the old trundle-bed! O the old trundle-bed!
With its plump little pillow, and old-fashioned
    spread;
Its snowy-white sheets, and the blankets above,
Smoothed down and tucked round with the touches
    of love;
The voice of my mother to lull me to sleep
With the old fairy stories my memories keep
Still fresh as the lilies that bloom o'er the head
Once bowed o'er my own in the old trundle-bed.

MY MARY

MY Mary, O my Mary!
　　The simmer skies are blue:
The dawnin' brings the dazzle,
　　An' the gloamin' brings the dew,—
The mirk o' nicht the glory
　　O' the moon, ar.' kindles, too,
The stars that shift aboon the lift.—
　　But naething brings me you!

Where is it, O my Mary,
　　Ye are biding a' the while?
I ha' wended by your window—
　　I ha' waited by the stile,
An' up an' down the river
　　I ha' won 'for mony a mile,
Yet never found, adrift or drown'd,
　　Your lang-belated smile.

Is it forgot, my Mary,
　　How glad we used to be?—
The simmer-time when bonny bloomed
　　The auld trysting-tree,—

How there I carved the name for you,
  An' you the name for me;
An' the gloamin' kenned it only
  When we kissed sae tenderly.

Speek ance to me, my Mary!—
  But whisper in my ear
As light as ony sleeper's breath,
  An' a' my soul will hear;
My heart shall stap its beating,
  An' the soughing atmosphere
Be hushed the while I leaning smile
  An' listen to you, dear!

My Mary, O my Mary!
  The blossoms bring the bees;
The sunshine brings the blossoms,
  An' the leaves on a' the trees;
The simmer brings the sunshine
  An' the fragrance o' the breeze,—
But O wi'out you, Mary,
  I care naething for these!

We were sae happy, Mary!
  O think how ance we said—
Wad ane o' us gae fickle,
  Or ane o' us lie dead,—
To feel anither's kisses
  We wad feign the auld instead,
An' ken the ither's footsteps
  In the green grass owerhead.

My Mary, O my Mary!
  Are ye dochter o' the air,
That ye vanish aye before me
  As I follow everywhere?—
Or is it ye are only
  But a mortal, wan wi' care,
Sin' I search through a' the kirkyird
  An' I dinna find ye there?

TWO SONNETS TO THE JUNE-BUG

I

YOU make me jes' a little nervouser
    Than any dog-gone bug I ever see!
  And you know night's the time to pester me—
When any tetch at all 'll rub the fur
Of all my patience back'ards! You're the myrrh
  And ruburb of my life! A bumblebee
  Cain't hold a candle to you; and a he
Bald hornet, with a laminated spur
In his hip-pocket, daresent even cheep
  When you're around! And, dern ye! you have made
Me lose whole ricks and stacks and piles of sleep,—
  And many of a livelong night I've laid
And never shut an eye, hearin' you keep
  Up that eternal buzzin' serenade!

II

And I've got up and lit the lamp, and clum
  On cheers and trunks and wash-stands and bu-
    reaus,
  And all such dangerous articles as those,

And biffed at you with brooms, and never come
'In two feet of you,—maybe skeered you some,—
   But what does that amount to when it throws
   A feller out o' balance, and his nose
Gits barked ag'inst the mantel, while you hum
Fer joy around the room, and churn your head
   Ag'inst the ceilin', and draw back and butt
The plasterin' loose, and drop—behind the bed,
   Where never human-bein' ever putt
Harm's hand on you, er ever truthful said
   He'd choked yer dern infernal wizzen shut!

ONE AFTERNOON

BELOW, cool grasses: over us
The maples waver tremulous.

A slender overture above,
Low breathing as a sigh of love

At first, then gradually strong
And stronger: 'tis the locust's song,

Swoln midway to a pæan of glee,
And lost in silence dwindlingly.

Not utter silence; nay, for hid
In ghosts of it, the katydid

Chirrs a diluted echo of
The loveless song he makes us love.

The low boughs are drugged heavily
With shade; the poem you read to me

Is not more gracious than the trill
Of birds that twitter as they will.

Half consciously, with upturned eyes,
I hear your voice—I see the skies,

Where, o'er bright rifts, the swallows glance
Like glad thoughts o'er a countenance;

And voices near and far are blent
Like sweet chords of some instrument

Awakened by the trembling touch
Of hands that love it overmuch.

Dear heart, let be the book a while!
I want your face—I want your smile!

Tell me how gladder now are they
Who look on us from Heaven to-day.

THE BEAUTIFUL CITY

THE Beautiful City! Forever
   Its rapturous praises resound;
We fain would behold it—but never
   A glimpse of its glory is found:
We slacken our lips at the tender
   White breasts of our mothers to hear
Of its marvelous beauty and splendor;—
   We see—but the gleam of a tear!

Yet never the story may tire us—
   First graven in symbols of stone—
Rewritten on scrolls of papyrus
   And parchment, and scattered and blown
By the winds of the tongues of all nations,
   Like a litter of leaves wildly whirled
Down the rack of a hundred translations,
   From the earliest lisp of the world.

We compass the earth and the ocean,
   From the Orient's uttermost light,
To where the last ripple in motion
   Lips hem of the skirt of the night,—

But the Beautiful City evades us—
    No spire of it glints in the sun—
No glad-bannered battlement shades us
    When all our long journey is done.

Where lies it? We question and listen;
    We lean from the mountain, or mast,
And see but dull earth, or the glisten
    Of seas inconceivably vast:
The dust of the one blurs our vision,
    The glare of the other our brain,
Nor city nor island Elysian
    In all of the land or the main!

We kneel in dim fanes where the thunders
    Of organs tumultuous roll,
And the longing heart listens and wonders,
    And the eyes look aloft from the soul:
But the chanson grows fainter and fainter,
    Swoons wholly away and is dead;
And our eyes only reach where the painter
    Has dabbled a saint overhead.

The Beautiful City! O mortal,
    Fare hopefully on in thy quest,
Pass down through the green grassy portal
    That leads to the Valley of Rest;
There first passed the One who, in pity
    Of all thy great yearning, awaits
To point out the Beautiful City,
    And loosen the trump at the gates.

A LIFE TERM

SHE was false, and he was true,—
    Thus their lives were rent apart;
'Twas his dagger driven through
    A mad rival's heart.

He was shut away. The moon
    May not find him; nor the stars—
Nay, nor yet the sun of noon
    Pierce his prison bars.

She was left—again to sin—
    Mistress of all siren arts:
The poor, soulless heroine
    Of a hundred hearts!

Though she dare not think of him
    Who believed her lies, and so
Sent a ghost adown the dim
    Path she dreads to go,—

He, in fancy, smiling, sips
    Of her kisses, purer yet
Than the dew upon the lips
    Of the violet.

McFEETERS' FOURTH

IT was needless to say 'twas a glorious day,
  And to boast of it all in that spread-eagle way
That our Forefathers had since the hour of the birth
Of this most patriotic republic on earth!
But 'twas justice, of course, to admit that the sight
Of the old Stars-and-Stripes was a thing of delight
In the eyes of a fellow, however he tried
To look on the day with a dignified pride
That meant not to brook any turbulent glee
Or riotous flourish of loud jubilee!

So argued McFeeters, all grim and severe,
Who the long night before, with a feeling of fear,
Had slumbered but fitfully, hearing the swish
Of the sky-rocket over his roof, with the wish
That the boy-fiend who fired it were fast to the end
Of the stick to forever and ever ascend!
Or to hopelessly ask why the boy with the horn
And its horrible havoc had ever been born!
Or to wish, in his wakefulness, staring aghast,
That this Fourth of July were as dead as the last!

So yesterday morning, McFeeters arose,
With a fire in his eyes, and a cold in his nose,
And a guttural voice in appropriate key
With a temper as gruff as a temper could be.
He growled at the servant he met on the stair,
Because he was whistling a national air,
And he growled at the maid on the balcony, who
Stood enrapt with the tune of "The Red-White-and-
        Blue"
That a band was discoursing like mad in the street,
With drumsticks that banged, and with cymbals that
        beat.

And he growled at his wife, as she buttoned his vest,
And applausively pinned a rosette on his breast
Of the national colors, and lured from his purse
Some change for the boys—for fire-crackers—or
        worse;
And she pointed with pride to a soldier in blue
In a frame on the wall, and the colors there, too;
And he felt, as he looked on the features, the glow
The painter found there twenty long years ago,
And a passionate thrill in his breast, as he felt
Instinctively round for the sword in his belt.

What was it that hung like a mist o'er the room?—
The tumult without—and the music—the boom
Of the cannon—the blare of the bugle and fife?—
No matter!—McFeeters was kissing his wife,
And laughing and crying and waving his hat

Like a genuine soldier, and crazy, at that!
—*Was* it needless to say 'twas a glorious day
And to boast of it all in that spread-eagle way
That our Forefathers had since the hour of the birth
Of this most patriotic republic on earth?

AT NINETY IN THE SHADE

HOT weather? Yes; but really not,
Compared with weather twice as hot.
Find comfort, then, in arguing thus,
And you'll pull through victorious!—
For instance, while you gasp and pant
And try to cool yourself—and can't—
With soda, cream and lemonade,
The heat at ninety in the shade,—
Just calmly sit and ponder o'er
These same degrees, with ninety more
On top of them, and so concede
The weather now is cool indeed!
Think—as the perspiration dews
Your fevered brow, and seems to ooze
From out the ends of every hair—
Whole floods of it, with floods to spare—
Think, I repeat, the while the sweat
Pours down your spine—how hotter yet
Just ninety *more* degrees would be,
And bear *this* ninety patiently!
Think—as you mop your brow and hair,
With sticky feelings everywhere—
How ninety more degrees increase

Of heat like this would start the grease;
Or, think, as you exhausted stand,
A wilted "palm-leaf" in each hand—
When the thermometer has done
With ease the lap of ninety-one;
O think, I say, what heat might do
At one hundred and eighty-two—
Just twice the heat you now declare,
Complainingly, is hard to bear.
Or, as you watch the mercury
Mount, still elate, one more degree,
And doff your collar and cravat,
And rig a sponge up in your hat,
And ask Tom, Harry, Dick or Jim
If this is hot enough for him—
Consider how the sun would pour
At one hundred and eighty-four—
Just twice the heat that seems to be
Affecting you unpleasantly,
The very hour that you might find
As cool as dew, were you inclined.
But why proceed when none will heed
Advice apportioned to the need?
Hot weather? Yes; but really not,
Compared with weather twice as hot!

And schoolgirl faces, pale and sweet,
Gleam from the shawls about their heads

A SUDDEN SHOWER

BAREFOOTED boys scud up the street
   Or skurry under sheltering sheds;
And schoolgirl faces, pale and sweet,
   Gleam from the shawls about their heads.

Doors bang; and mother-voices call
   From alien homes; and rusty gates
Are slammed; and high above it all,
   The thunder grim reverberates.

And then, abrupt,—the rain! the rain!—
   The earth lies gasping; and the eyes
Behind the streaming window-pane
   Smile at the trouble of the skies.

The highway smokes; sharp echoes ring;
   The cattle bawl and cow-bells clank;
And into town comes galloping
   The farmer's horse, with steaming flank.

The swallow dips beneath the eaves
   And flirts his plumes and folds his wings;
And under the Catawba leaves
   The caterpillar curls and clings.

The bumblebee is pelted down
    The wet stem of the hollyhock;
And sullenly, in spattered brown,
    The cricket leaps the garden-walk.

Within, the baby claps his hands
    And crows with rapture strange and
        vague;
Without, beneath the rose-bush stands
    A dripping rooster on one leg.

GOOD-BY ER HOWDY-DO

SAY good-by er howdy-do—
   What's the odds betwixt the two?
Comin'—goin', ev'ry day—
Best friends first to go away—
Grasp of hands you'd ruther hold
Than their weight in solid gold
Slips their grip while greetin' you.—
Say good-by er howdy-do!

Howdy-do, and then, good-by—
Mixes jes' like laugh and cry;
Deaths and births, and worst and best,
Tangled their contrariest;
Ev'ry jinglin' weddin'-bell
Skeerin' up some funer'l knell.—
Here's my song, and there's your sigh.—
Howdy-do, and then, good-by!

Say good-by er howdy-do—
Jes' the same to me and you;
'Taint worth while to make no fuss,
'Cause the job's put up on us!
Some One's runnin' this concern
That's got nothin' else to learn:
Ef *He's* willin', we'll pull through—
Say good-by er howdy-do!

WITH THE CURRENT

RAREST mood of all the year!
  Aimless, idle, and content—
Sky and wave and atmosphere
    Wholly indolent.

Little daughter, loose the band
  From your tresses—let them pour
Shadow-like o'er arm and hand
    Idling at the oar.

Low and clear, and pure and deep,
  Ripples of the river sing—
Water-lilies, half asleep,
    Drowsed with listening:

Tremulous reflex of skies—
  Skies above and skies below,—
Paradise and Paradise
    Blending even so!

Blossoms with their leaves unrolled
  Laughingly, as they were lips
Cleft with ruddy beaten gold
    Tongues of pollen-tips.

Rush and reed, and thorn and vine,
  Clumped with grasses lithe and tall—
With a web of summer-shine
    Woven round it all.

Back and forth, and to and fro—
  Flashing scale and wing as one,—
Dragon-flies that come and go,
    Shuttled by the sun.

Fairy lilts and lullabies,
  Fine as fantasy conceives,—
Echoes wrought of cricket-cries
    Sifted through the leaves.

O'er the rose, with drowsy buzz,
  Hangs the bee, and stays his kiss,
Even as my fancy does,
    Gipsy, over this.

Let us both be children—share
  Youth's glad voyage night and day,
Drift adown it, half aware,
    Anywhere we may.—

Drift and curve and deviate,
  Veer and eddy, float and flow,
Waver, swerve and undulate,
    As the bubbles go.

D—7

WET-WEATHER TALK

IT hain't no use to grumble and complane;
   It's jest as cheap and easy to rejoice.—
When God sorts out the weather and sends
         rain,
   W'y, rain's my choice.

Men ginerly, to all intents—
   Although they're apt to grumble some—
Puts most theyr trust in Providence,
   And takes things as they come—
      That is, the commonality
      Of men that's lived as long as me
      Has watched the world enugh to learn
      They're not the boss of this concern.

With *some*, of course, it's different—
   I've saw *young* men that knowed it all,
And didn't like the way things went
   On this terrestchul ball;—
      But all the same, the rain, some way,
      Rained jest as hard on picnic day;
      Er, when they railly *wanted* it,
      It maybe wouldn't rain a bit!

948

In this existunce, dry and wet
　　Will overtake the best of men—
Some little skift o' clouds'll shet
　　The sun off now and then.—
　　　　And mayby, whilse you're wundern who
　　　　You've fool-like lent your umbrell' to,
　　　　And *want* it—out'll pop the sun,
　　　　And you'll be glad you hain't got none!

It aggervates the farmers, too—
　　They's too much wet, er too much sun,
Er work, er waitin' round to do
　　Before the plowin' 's done:
　　　　And mayby, like as not, the wheat,
　　　　Jest as it's lookin' hard to beat,
　　　　Will ketch the storm—and jest about
　　　　The time the corn's a-jintin' out.

These-here *cy-clones* a-foolin' round—
　　And back'ard crops!—and wind and rain!—
And yit the corn that's wallerd down
　　May elbow up again!—
　　　　They hain't no sense, as I can see,
　　　　Fer mortuls, sich as us, to be
　　　　A-faultin' Natchur's wise intents,
　　　　And lockin' horns with Providence!

It hain't no use to grumble and complane;
　　It's jest as cheap and easy to rejoice.—
When God sorts out the weather and sends rain,
　　　　W'y, rain's my choice.

A POOR MAN'S WEALTH

A POOR man? Yes, I must confess—
No wealth of gold do I possess;
No pastures fine, with grazing kine,
Nor fields of waving grain are mine;
No foot of fat or fallow land
Where rightfully my feet may stand
The while I claim it as my own—
By deed and title, mine alone.

Ah, poor indeed! perhaps you say—
But spare me your compassion, pray!—
When I ride not—with you—I walk
In Nature's company, and talk
With one who will not slight or slur
The child forever dear to her—
And one who answers back, be sure,
With smile for smile, though I am poor.

And while communing thus, I count
An inner wealth of large amount,—
The wealth of honest purpose blent
With Penury's environment,—
The wealth of owing naught to-day
But debts that I would gladly pay,
With wealth of thanks still unexpressed
With cumulative interest.—

A wealth of patience and content—
For all my ways improvident;
A faith still fondly exercised—
For all my plans unrealized;
A wealth of promises that still,
Howe'er I fail, I hope to fill;
A wealth of charity for those
Who pity me my ragged clothes.

A poor man? Yes, I must confess—
No wealth of gold do I possess;
No pastures fine, with grazing kine,
Nor fields of waving grain are mine;
But ah, my friend! I've wealth, no end!
For millionairies might condescend
To bend the knee and envy me
This opulence of poverty.

AUTOGRAPHIC

For an Album

I FEEL, if aught I ought to rhyme,
I ought 'a' thought a longer time,
And ought 'a' caught a higher sense,
Of autocratic eloquence.
I ought 'a' sought each haughty Muse
That taught a thought I ought to use,
And fought and fraught, and so devised
A poem *unmonotonized.*—
But since all this was vain, I thought
I ought to simply say,—I ought
To thank you, as I ought to do,
And ought to bow my best to you;
And ought to trust not to intrude
A rudely-wrought-up gratitude,
But ought to smile, and ought to laugh,
And ought to write—an autograph.

IN SWIMMING-TIME

CLOUDS above, as white as wool,
    Drifting over skies as blue
As the eyes of beautiful
    Children when they smile at you;
Groves of maple, elm, and beech,
    With the sunshine sifted through
Branches, mingling each with each,
    Dim with shade and bright with dew;
Stripling trees, and poplars hoar,
Hickory and sycamore,
And the drowsy dogwood bowed
Where the ripples laugh aloud,
And the crooning creek is stirred
    To a gaiety that now
Mates the warble of the bird
    Teetering on the hazel-bough;
Grasses long and fine and fair
As your schoolboy sweetheart's hair,
Backward roached and twirled and twined
By the fingers of the wind.
Vines and mosses, interlinked
    Down dark aisles and deep ravines,
Where the stream runs, willow-brinked,

Round a bend where some one leans
Faint and vague and indistinct
  As the like reflected thing
  In the current shimmering.
Childish voices farther on,
Where the truant stream has gone,
Vex the echoes of the wood
Till no word is understood,
Save that one is well aware
Happiness is hiding there.
There, in leafy coverts, nude
  Little bodies poise and leap,
Spattering the solitude
And the silence everywhere—
  Mimic monsters of the deep!
Wallowing in sandy shoals—
  Plunging headlong out of sight;
  And, with spurtings of delight,
Clutching hands, and slippery soles,
  Climbing up the treacherous steep
Over which the spring-board spurns
Each again as he returns.
  Ah! the glorious carnival!
    Purple lips and chattering teeth—
    Eyes that burn—but, in beneath,
  Every care beyond recall,
    Every task forgotten quite—
    And again, in dreams at night,
  Dropping, drifting through it all!

THE BEST IS GOOD ENOUGH

I QUARREL not with Destiny,
  But make the best of everything—
The best is good enough for me.

Leave Discontent alone, and she
Will shut her mouth and let *you* sing.
I quarrel not with Destiny.

I take some things, or let 'em be—
Good gold has always got the ring;
The best is good enough for me.

Since Fate insists on secrecy,
I have no arguments to bring—
I quarrel not with Destiny.

The fellow that goes "haw" for "gee"
Will find he hasn't got full swing.
The best is good enough for me.

One only knows our needs, and He
Does all of the distributing.
I quarrel not with Destiny:
The best is good enough for me.

HE CALLED HER IN

I

HE called her in from me and shut the door.
  And she so loved the sunshine and the
      sky!—
She loved them even better yet than I
That ne'er knew dearth of them—my mother
    dead,
Nature had nursed me in her lap instead:
And I had grown a dark and eery child
That rarely smiled,
Save when, shut all alone in grasses high,
Looking straight up in God's great lonesome sky
And coaxing Mother to smile back on me.
'Twas lying thus, this fair girl suddenly
Came on me, nestled in the fields beside
A pleasant-seeming home, with doorway wide—
The sunshine beating in upon the floor
Like golden rain.—
O sweet, sweet face above me, turn again
And leave me! I had cried, but that an ache
Within my throat so gripped it I could make
No sound but a thick sobbing. Cowering so,
I felt her light hand laid
Upon my hair—a touch that ne'er before

Had tamed me thus, all soothed and unafraid—
It seemed the touch the children used to know
When Christ was here, so dear it was—so dear,—
At once I loved her as the leaves love dew
In midmost summer when the days are new.
Barely an hour I knew her, yet a curl
Of silken sunshine did she clip for me
Out of the bright May-morning of her hair,
And bound and gave it to me laughingly,
And caught my hands and called me *"Little girl,"*
Tiptoeing, as she spoke, to kiss me there!
And I stood dazed and dumb for very stress
Of my great happiness.

She plucked me by the gown, nor saw how mean
The raiment—drew me with her everywhere:
Smothered her face in tufts of grasses green:
Put up her dainty hands and peeped between
Her fingers at the blossoms—crooned and talked
To them in strange, glad whispers, as we
    walked,—
Said *this* one was her angel mother—*this,*
Her baby-sister—come back, for a kiss,
Clean from the Good-World!—smiled and kissed
    them, then
Closed her soft eyes and kissed them o'er again,
And so did she beguile me—so we played,—
She was the dazzling Shine—I, the dark Shade—
And we did mingle like to these, and thus,
Together, made
The perfect summer, pure and glorious.
So blent we, till a harsh voice broke upon

Our happiness.—She, startled as a fawn,
Cried, "Oh, 'tis Father!"—all the blossoms gone
From out her cheeks as those from out her
    grasp.—
Harsher the voice came:—She could only gasp
Affrightedly, "Good-by!—good-by! good-by!"
And lo, I stood alone, with that harsh cry
Ringing a new and unknown sense of shame
Through soul and frame,
And, with wet eyes, repeating o'er and o'er,—
"He called her in from me and shut the door!"

II

He called her in from me and shut the door!
And I went wandering alone again—
So lonely—O so very lonely then,
I thought no little sallow star, alone
In all a world of twilight, e'er had known
Such utter loneliness. But that I wore
Above my heart that gleaming tress of hair
To lighten up the night of my despair,
I think I might have groped into my grave
Nor cared to wave
The ferns above it with a breath of prayer.
And how I hungered for the sweet, sweet face
That bent above me in my hiding-place
That day amid the grasses there beside
Her pleasant home!—"Her *pleasant* home!" I
    sighed,
Remembering;—then shut my teeth and feigned

The harsh voice calling *me*,—then clenched my
    nails
So deeply in my palms, the sharp wounds pained,
And tossed my face toward Heaven, as one who
    pales
In splendid martyrdom, with soul serene,
As near to God as high the guillotine.
And I had *envied* her? Not that—O no!
But I had longed for some sweet haven so!—
Wherein the tempest-beaten heart might ride
Sometimes at peaceful anchor, and abide
Where those that loved me touched me with their
    hands,
And looked upon me with glad eyes, and slipped
Smooth fingers o'er my brow, and lulled the
    strands
Of my wild tresses, as they backward tipped
My yearning face and kissed it satisfied.
Then bitterly I murmured as before,—
"He called her in from me and shut the door!"

III

He called her in from me and shut the door!
After long struggling with my pride and pain—
A weary while it seemed, in which the more
I held myself from her, the greater fain
Was I to look upon her face again;—
At last—at last—half conscious where my feet
Were faring, I stood waist-deep in the sweet
Green grasses there where she

First came to me.—
The very blossoms she had plucked that day,
And, at her father's voice, had cast away,
Around me lay,
Still bright and blooming in these eyes of mine;
And as I gathered each one eagerly,
I pressed it to my lips and drank the wine
Her kisses left there for the honey-bee.
Then, after I had laid them with the tress
Of her bright hair with lingering tenderness,
I, turning, crept on to the hedge that bound
Her pleasant-seeming home—but all around
Was never sign of her!—The windows all
Were blinded; and I heard no rippling fall
Of her glad laugh, nor any harsh voice call;—
But, clutching to the tangled grasses, caught
A sound as though a strong man bowed his head
And sobbed alone—unloved—uncomforted!—
And then straightway before
My tearless eyes, all vividly, was wrought
A vision that is with me evermore:—
A little girl that lies asleep, nor hears
Nor heeds not any voice nor fall of tears.—
And I sit singing o'er and o'er and o'er,—
"God called her in from him and shut the door!"

GIVE ME THE BABY

GIVE me the baby to hold, my dear—
  To hold and hug, and to love and kiss.
Ah! he will come to me, never a fear—
  Come to the nest of a breast like this,
As warm for him as his face with cheer.
Give me the baby to hold, my dear!

Trustfully yield him to my caress.
  "Bother," you say? What! "a bother" to
    me?—
To fill up my soul with such happiness
  As the love of a baby that laughs to be
Snuggled away where my heart can hear!
Give me the baby to hold, my dear!

Ah, but his hands are grimed, you say,
  And would soil my laces and clutch my hair.—
Well, what would pleasure me more, I pray,
  Than the touch and tug of the wee hands
      there?—
The wee hands there, and the warm face here—
Give me the baby to hold, my dear!

Give me the baby! (Oh, won't you see?
   . . . Somewhere, out where the green of
      the lawn
Is turning to gray, and the maple tree
  Is weeping its leaves of gold upon
A little mound, with a dead rose near. . . .)
Give me the baby to hold, my dear!

AN AUTUMNAL TONIC

WHAT mystery is it? The morning as rare
    As the Indian Summer may bring!
A tang in the frost and a spice in the air
    That no city poet can sing!
The crimson and amber and gold of the leaves,
    As they loosen and flutter and fall
In the path of the park, as it rustlingly weaves
Its way through the maples and under the eaves
    Of the sparrows that chatter and call.

What hint of delight is it tingles me through?—
    What vague, indefinable joy?
What yearning for something divine that I knew
    When a wayward and wood-roving boy?
Ah-ha! and Oho! but I have it, I say—
    Oh, the mystery brightens at last,—
'Tis the longing and zest of the far, far away,
For a bountiful, old-fashioned dinner to-day,
    With the hale harvest-hands of the past.

OUT OF THE HITHERWHERE

OUT of the hitherwhere into the YON—
The land that the Lord's love rests upon;
Where one may rely on the friends he meets,
And the smiles that greet him along the streets:
Where the mother that left you years ago
Will lift the hands that were folded so,
And put them about you, with all the love
And tenderness you are dreaming of.

Out of the hitherwhere into the YON—
Where all of the friends of your youth have gone,—
Where the old schoolmate that laughed with you,
Will laugh again as he used to do,
Running to meet you, with such a face
As lights like a moon the wondrous place
Where God is living, and glad to live,
Since He is the Master and may forgive.

Out of the hitherwhere into the YON!—
Stay the hopes we are leaning on—
You, Divine, with Your merciful eyes
Looking down from the far-away skies,—
Smile upon us, and reach and take
Our worn souls Home for the old home's sake.—
And so Amen,—for our all seems gone
Out of the hitherwhere into the YON.

A TINKLE OF BELLS

THE light of the moon on the white of the snow,
  And the answering twinkles along the street,
And our sleigh flashing by, in the glamour and
    glow
Of the glorious nights of the long ago,
  When the laugh of her lips rang clear and sweet
As the tinkle our horses shook out of the bells
  And flung and tossed back
  On our glittering track
In a shower of tremulous, murmuring swells
  Of the echoing, airy, melodious bells!—
  O the mirth of the bells!
  And the worth of the bells!
  Come tinkle again, in this dearth of the bells,
The laughter and love that I lack, yearning back
  For the far-away sound of the bells!

Ah! the bells, they were glad in the long ago!
And the tinkles they had, they have thrilled me so
I have said: "It is they and her songs and face
Make summer for me of the wintriest place!"
And now—but sobbings and sad farewells,
  As I peer in the night through the sleeted pane,
Hearing a clangor and wrangle of bells,
  And never a tinkle again!

The snow is a-swoon, and the moon dead-white,
And the frost is wild in the air to-night!
    Yet still will I linger and listen and pray
    Till the sound of her voice shall come this way,
        With a tinkle of bells,
            And the lisp-like tread
                Of the hooves of the sleigh,
        And the murmurs and swells
            Of the vows she said.
    And oh, I shall listen as madmen may,
Till the tinkling bells ring down this way!—
Till again the grasp of my hand entwines
The tensioned loops of the quivering lines,
And again we ride in the wake of the pride
And the strength of the coursers, side by side,
With our faces smitten again by the spray
Of the froth of our steeds as we gallop away
    In affright of the bells,
    And the might of the bells,
And the infinite glee and delight of the bells,
As they tinkle and tinkle and tinkle, till they
Are heard through the dawn where the mists are
        drawn,
And we canter and gallop and dash away
    Sheer into The Judgment Day!

THE OLD MAN

LO! steadfast and serene,
　　In patient pause between
The seen and the unseen,
　　What gentle zephyrs fan
Your silken silver hair,—
And what diviner air
Breathes round you like a prayer,
　　　　Old Man?

Can you, in nearer view
Of Glory, pierce the blue
Of happy Heaven through;
　　And, listening mutely, can
Your senses, dull to us,
Hear Angel-voices thus,
In chorus glorious—
　　　　Old Man?

In your reposeful gaze
The dusk of Autumn days
Is blent with April haze,
　　As when of old began

The bursting of the bud
Of rosy babyhood—
When all the world was good,
　　Old Man.

And yet I find a sly
Little twinkle in your eye;
And your whisperingly shy
　　Little laugh is simply an
Internal shout of glee
That betrays the fallacy
You'd perpetrate on me,
　　Old Man!

So just put up the frown
That your brows are pulling down!
Why, the fleetest boy in town,
　　As he bared his feet and ran,
Could read with half a glance—
And of keen rebuke, perchance—
Your secret countenance,
　　Old Man!

Now, honestly, confess:
Is an old man any less
Than the little child we bless
　　And caress when we can?
Isn't age but just a place
Where you mask the childish face
To preserve its inner grace,
　　Old Man?

Hasn't age a truant day,
Just as that you went astray
In the wayward, restless way,
When, brown with dust and tan,
Your roguish face essayed,
In solemn masquerade,
To hide the smile it made,
Old Man?

Now, fair, and square, and true,
Don't your old soul tremble through,
As in youth it used to do
When it brimmed and overran
With the strange, enchanted sights,
And the splendors and delights
Of the old "Arabian Nights,"
Old Man?

When, haply, you have fared
Where glad Aladdin shared
His lamp with you, and dared
The Afrite and his clan;
And, with him, clambered through
The trees where jewels grew—
And filled your pockets, too,
Old Man?

Or, with Sinbad, at sea—
And in veracity
Who has sinned as bad as he,
Or would, or will, or can?—

Have you listened to his lies,
With open mouth and eyes,
And learned his art likewise,
  Old Man?

And you need not deny
That your eyes were wet as dry,
Reading novels on the sly!
  And review them, if you can
And the same warm tears will fall—
Only faster, that is all—
Over Little Nell and Paul,
  Old Man!

Oh, you were a lucky lad—
Just as good as you were bad!
And the host of friends you had—
  Charley, Tom, and Dick, and Dan;
And the old School-Teacher, too,
Though he often censured you;
And the girls in pink and blue,
  Old Man.

And—as often you have leant,
In boyish sentiment,
To kiss the letter sent
  By Nelly, Belle, or Nan—
Wherein the rose's hue
Was red, the violet blue—
And sugar sweet—and you,
  Old Man,—

So, to-day, as lives the bloom,
And the sweetness, and perfume
Of the blossoms, I assume,
    On the same mysterious plan
The Master's love assures,
That the selfsame boy endures
In that hale old heart of yours,
    Old Man.

OUR KIND OF A MAN

I

THE kind of a man for you and me!
  He faces the world unflinchingly,
And smites, as long as the wrong resists,
With a knuckled faith and force like fists:
He lives the life he is preaching of,
And loves where most is the need of love;
His voice is clear to the deaf man's ears,
And his face sublime through the blind man's tears;
The light shines out where the clouds were dim,
And the widow's prayer goes up for him;
The latch is clicked at the hovel door
And the sick man sees the sun once more,
And out o'er the barren fields he sees
Springing blossoms and waving trees,
Feeling as only the dying may,
That God's own servant has come that way,
Smoothing the path as it still winds on
Through the golden gate where his loved have gone.

II

The kind of a man for me and you!
However little of worth we do
He credits full, and abides in trust
That time will teach us how more is just.
He walks abroad, and he meets all kinds
Of querulous and uneasy minds,
And, sympathizing, he shares the pain
Of the doubts that rack us, heart and brain;
And, knowing this, as we grasp his hand,
We are surely coming to understand!
He looks on sin with pitying eyes—
E'en as the Lord, since Paradise,—
Else, should we read, Though our sins should glow
As scarlet, they shall be white as snow?—
And, feeling still, with a grief half glad,
That the bad are as good as the good are bad,
He strikes straight out for the Right—and he
Is the kind of a man for you and me!

THE LITTLE COAT

HERE'S his ragged "roundabout." . .
Turn the pockets inside out:
See; his penknife, lost to use,
Rusted shut with apple-juice;
Here, with marbles, top and string,
Is his deadly "devil-sling,"
With its rubber, limp at last
As the sparrows of the past!
Beeswax—buckles—leather straps—
Bullets, and a box of caps,—
Not a thing of all, I guess,
But betrays some waywardness—
E'en these tickets, blue and red,
For the Bible-verses said—
Such as this his mem'ry kept,—
                    "Jesus wept."

Here's a fishing-hook and -line,
Tangled up with wire and twine,
And dead angleworms, and some
Slugs of lead and chewing-gum,
Blent with scents that can but come
From the oil of rhodium.

Here—a soiled, yet dainty note,
That some little sweetheart wrote,
Dotting—"Vine grows round the stump,"
And—"My sweetest sugar-lump!"
Wrapped in this—a padlock key
Where he's filed a touch-hole—see!
And some powder in a quill
Corked up with a liver pill;
And a spongy little chunk
    Of "punk."

Here's the little coat—but O
Where is he we've censured so?
Don't you hear us calling, dear?
Back! come back, and never fear.—
You may wander where you will,
Over orchard, field and hill;
You may kill the birds, or do
Anything that pleases you!
Ah, this empty coat of his!
Every tatter worth a kiss;
Every stain as pure instead
As the white stars overhead:
And the pockets—homes were they
Of the little hands that play
Now no more—but, absent, thus
    Beckon us.

AN IMPROMPTU ON ROLLER SKATES

RUMBLE, tumble, growl and grate!
  Skip, and trip, and gravitate!
Lunge, and plunge, and thrash the planks
With your blameless, shameless shanks:
In excruciating pain,
Stand upon your head again,
And, uncoiling kink by kink,
Kick the roof out of the rink!

In derisive bursts of mirth,
Drop ka-whop and jar the earth!
Jolt your lungs down in your socks,
Oh! tempestuous equinox
Of dismembered legs and arms!
Strew your ways with wild alarms;
Fameward skoot and ricochet
On your glittering vertebrae!

ME AND MARY

ALL my feelin's in the Spring
 Gits so blame contrary,
I can't think of anything
 Only me and Mary!
"Me and Mary!" all the time,
"Me and Mary!" like a rhyme,
Keeps a-dingin' on till I'm
 Sick o' "Me and Mary!"

"Me and Mary! Ef us two
 Only was together—
Playin' like we used to do
 In the Aprile weather!"
All the night and all the day
I keep wishin' thataway
Till I'm gittin' old and gray
 Jes' on "Me and Mary!"

Muddy yit along the pike
 Sence the Winter's freezin',
And the orchard's back'ard-like
 Bloomin' out this season;

Only heerd one bluebird yit—
Nary robin ner tomtit;
What's the how and why of it?
    'Spect it's "Me and Mary!"

Me and Mary liked the birds—
    That is, *Mary* sort o'
Liked 'em first, and afterwards,
    W'y, I thought *I'd* ort 'o.
And them birds—ef Mary stood
Right here with me, like she should—
They'd be singin', them birds would,
    All fer me and Mary.

Birds er not, I'm hopin' some
    I can git to plowin'!
Ef the sun'll only come,
    And the Lord allowin',
Guess to-morry I'll turn in
And git down to work ag'in;
This here loaferin' won't win,
    Not fer me and Mary!

Fer a man that loves, like me,
    And's afeard to name it,
Till some other feller, he
    Gits the girl—dad-shame-it!
Wet er dry, er cloud er sun—
Winter gone er jes' begun—
Outdoor work fer me er none,
    No more "Me and Mary!"

"Me and Mary"

WRITTEN IN BUNNER'S "AIRS FROM ARCADY"

O EVER gracious Airs from Arcady!
    What lack is there of any jocund thing
  In glancing wit or glad imagining
Capricious fancy may not find in thee?—
The laugh of Momus, tempered daintily
  To lull the ear and lure its listening;
  The whistled syllables the birds of spring
Flaunt ever at our guessings what they be;
The wood, the seashore, and the clanging town;
  The pets of fashion, and the ways of such;
  The *robe de chambre,* and the russet gown;
  The lordling's carriage, and the pilgrim's crutch—
From hale old Chaucer's wholesomeness, clean
    down
  To our artistic Dobson's deftest touch!

A SONG

THERE is ever a song somewhere, my dear;
  There is ever a something sings alway:
There's the song of the lark when the skies are
    clear,
  And the song of the thrush when the skies are
    gray.
The sunshine showers across the grain,
  And the bluebird trills in the orchard tree;
And in and out, when the eaves drip rain,
  The swallows are twittering ceaselessly.

There is ever a song somewhere, my dear,
  Be the skies above or dark or fair,
There is ever a song that our hearts may hear—
There is ever a song somewhere, my dear—
  There is ever a song somewhere!

There is ever a song somewhere, my dear,
  In the midnight black, or the midday blue:
The robin pipes when the sun is here,
  And the cricket chirrups the whole night through.
The buds may blow, and the fruit may grow,
  And the autumn leaves drop crisp and sear;
But whether the sun, or the rain, or the snow,
  There is ever a song somewhere, my dear.

There is ever a song somewhere, my dear,
  Be the skies above or dark or fair,
There is ever a song that our hearts may hear—
There is ever a song somewhere, my dear—
  There is ever a song somewhere!

NEVER TALK BACK

NEVER talk back! sich things is repperhensible;
    A feller only hurts hisse'f that jaws a man
        that's hot;
In a quarrel, ef you'll only keep your mouth shet
        and act sensible,
    The man that does the talkin' 'll git worsted every
        shot!

Never talk back to a feller that's abusin' you—
    Jes' let him carry on, and rip, and snort, and
        swear;
And when he finds his blamin' and defamin' 's jes'
        amusin' you,
    You've got him clean kaflummixed,—and you
        want to hold him there!

Never talk back, and wake up the whole community
    And call a man a liar, over Law, er Politics.—
You can lift and land him furder and with grace-
        fuller impunity
    With one good jolt of silence than a half a dozen
        kicks!

MY FRIEND

"He is my friend," I said,—
    "Be patient!" Overhead
The skies were drear and dim;
And lo! the thought of him
Smiled on my heart—and then
The sun shone out again!

"He is my friend!" The words
Brought summer and the birds;
And all my winter-time
Thawed into running rhyme
And rippled into song,
Warm, tender, brave, and strong.

And so it sings to-day.—
So may it sing alway!
Though waving grasses grow
Between, and lilies blow
Their trills of perfume clear
As laughter to the ear,
Let each mute measure end
With "Still he is thy friend."

THE LITTLE FAT DOCTOR

H E seemed so strange to me, every way—
    In manner, and form, and size,
From the boy I knew but yesterday,—
    I could hardly believe my eyes!

To hear his name called over there,
    My memory thrilled with glee
And leaped to picture him young and fair
    In youth, as he used to be.

But looking, only as glad eyes can,
    For the boy I knew of yore,
I smiled on a portly little man
    I had never seen before!—

Grave as a judge in courtliness—
    Professor-like and bland—
A little fat doctor and nothing less,
    With his hat in his kimboed hand.

But how we talked old times, and "chaffed"
    Each other with "Minnie," and "Jim"—
And how the little fat doctor laughed,
    And how I laughed with him!

"And it's pleasant," I thought, "though I
    yearn to see
  The face of the youth that was,
To know no boy could smile on me
  As the little fat doctor does!"

THE STRANGE YOUNG MAN

'TWAS a strange young man of the dreamy times
When bards made money, and bankers rhymes;
And drones made honey—and bees made naught;
And the bad sung hymns, and the good-folk fought;
And the merchants lurked in the shade all day
And pitched horseshoes in a listless way!
When the ticket-man at the station knew
If your trunk would go if you checked it through,
And if 2:30 meant half-past two,
And what in-the-name-of-the-land to do
If a man got left when he oughtn't to:
When the cabman wept as he took your fare,
And the street-car driver led in prayer—
And the cuss with the dyed mustache was there
That rode in town on a "jumper"-sled,
And got whipped twice for the things he said
To fellows that told him his hair was red.
And the strange young man (of which and whom
Our pencil offers to deign presume
To treat of now, in the days like these
When young men dress as they please to please)
Went round in a coat of pale pink-blue,

And a snow-white vest of a crimson hue,
And trousers purple, and gaiters gray—
All cut, as the French or the Dutch would say,—
La—macht nichts aus, oder—décolleté,—
Strange not only in dress, but in
The dimples he wore in cheek and chin—
All nailed over with scraps of tin,
Where he hadn't been shaved as he'd ought o'
    been;—
And his crape cravat, and the shape of that,
And the ear-tab over his diamond-pin.
And his friends all wondered, and used to say,—
"What a strange young man! Ah me! Hooray!
How sad he seems in his wild delight!
And how tickled indeed when he weeps outright!
What a comical man when he writhes in pain;
And how grieved he grows when he's glad again!"
And marveling still to remark new facts,
They said, "How slender and slim he acts!
And isn't it odd for a man to wear
A thumb-stall over his nose, and pare
His finger-nails with a carving-knife,
And talk of prunes to the landlord's wife?
It is patent to us—and, indeed, no doubt,
    Though as safely sealed as an oyster-can,—
Our interest in him must needs leak out,—
    Namely, that he is a strange young man!"

SCOTTY

SCOTTY'S dead.—Of course he is!
Jes' that same old luck of his!—
Ever sence we went cahoots
He's be'n first, you bet yer boots!
When our schoolin' first begun,
Got two whippin's to my one:
Stold and smoked the first cigar:
Stood up first before the bar,
Takin' whisky-straight—and me
Wastin' time on "blackberry"!
Beat me in the Army, too,
And clean on the whole way through!—
In more scrapes around the camp,
And more troubles, on the tramp:
Fought and fell there by my side
With more bullets in his hide,
And more glory in the cause,—
That's the kind o' man *he* was!
Luck liked Scotty more'n me.—
I got married: Scotty, he
Never even would *apply*
Fer the pension-money I
Had to beg of "Uncle Sam"—

That's the kind o' cuss *I* am!—
Scotty allus first and best—
Me the last and ornriest!
Yit fer all that's said and done—
All the battles fought and won—
We hain't prospered, him ner me—
Both as pore as pore could be,—
Though we've allus, up tel now,
Stuck together anyhow—
Scotty allus, as I've said,
Luckiest—And now he's *dead!*

ON THE SUNNY SIDE

HI and whoop-hooray, boys!
　　Sing a song of cheer!
Here's a holiday, boys,
　　Lasting half a year!
Round the world, and half is
　　Shadow we have tried;
Now we're where the laugh is,—
　　On the sunny side!

Pigeons coo and mutter,
　　Strutting high aloof
Where the sunbeams flutter
　　Through the stable roof.
Hear the chickens cheep, boys,
　　And the hen with pride
Clucking them to sleep, boys,
　　On the sunny side!

Hear the clacking guinea;
　　Hear the cattle moo;
Hear the horses whinny,
　　Looking out at you!

990

On the hitching-block, boys,
  Grandly satisfied,
See the old peacock, boys,
  On the sunny side!

Robins in the peach tree;
  Bluebirds in the pear;
Blossoms over each tree
  In the orchard there!
All the world's in joy, boys,
  Glad and glorified
As a romping boy, boys,
  On the sunny side!

Where's a heart as mellow—
  Where's a soul as free—
Where is any fellow
  We would rather be?
Just ourselves or none, boys,
  World around and wide,
Laughing in the sun, boys,
  On the sunny side!

THE HARPER

LIKE a drift of faded blossoms
  Caught in a slanting rain,
His fingers glimpsed down the strings of
    his harp
  In a tremulous refrain:

Patter and tinkle, and drip and drip!
  Ah! but the chords were rainy sweet!
And I closed my eyes and I bit my lip,
  As he played there in the street.

Patter, and drip, and tinkle!
  And there was the little bed
In the corner of the garret,
  And the rafters overhead!

And there was the little window—
  Tinkle, and drip, and drip!—
The rain above, and a mother's love,
  And God's companionship!

THE BLOSSOMS ON THE TREES

BLOSSOMS crimson, white, or blue,
  Purple, pink, and every hue,
From sunny skies, to tintings drowned
    In dusky drops of dew,
I praise you all, wherever found,
    And love you through and through;—
      But, Blossoms on the Trees,
        With your breath upon the breeze,
There's nothing all the world around
    As half as sweet as you!

Could the rhymer only wring
  All the sweetness to the lees
Of all the kisses clustering
    In juicy Used-to-bes,
To dip his rhymes therein and sing
    The blossoms on the trees,—
"O Blossoms on the Trees,"
  He would twitter, trill, and coo,
"However sweet, such songs as these
    Are not as sweet as you:—
For you are *blooming* melodies
    The *eyes* may listen to!"

993

LAUGHTER HOLDING BOTH HIS SIDES

AY, thou varlet! Laugh away!
    All the world's a holiday!
Laugh away, and roar and shout
Till thy hoarse tongue lolleth out!
Bloat thy cheeks, and bulge thine eyes
Unto bursting; pelt thy thighs
With thy swollen palms, and roar
As thou never hast before!
Lustier! wilt thou! peal on peal!
Stiflest? Squat and grind thy heel—
Wrestle with thy loins, and then
Wheeze thee whiles, and whoop again!

IN STATE

IS it the martins or katydids?—
Early morning or late at night?
A dream, belike, kneeling down on the lids
Of a dying man's eyesight.

.   .   .   .

Over and over I heard the rain—
Over and over I waked to see
The blaze of the lamp as again and again
Its stare insulted me.

.   .   .   .

It is not the click of the clock I hear—
It is the *pulse* of the clock,—and lo!
How it throbs and throbs on the quickened ear
Of the dead man listening so!

I heard them whisper *"She* would not come;"
But, being dead, I knew—I knew! . . .
Some hearts they love us alive, and some
They love us dead—they do!

995

And *I* am dead—and I joy to be,—
  For here are my folded hands, so cold,
And yet blood-warm with the roses she
  Has given me to hold.

Dead—yea, dead!—But I hear the beat
  Of her heart, as her warm lips touch my
      brow—
And O how sweet—how *blinding* sweet
  To know that she loves me *now!*

THE DEAD LOVER

TIME is so long when a man is dead!
  Some one sews; and the room is made
Very clean; and the light is shed
  Soft through the window-shade.

Yesterday I thought: "I know
  Just how the bells will sound, and how
The friends will talk, and the sermon go,
  And the hearse-horse bow and bow!"

This is to-day; and I have no thing
  To think of—nothing whatever to do
But to hear the throb of the pulse of a wing
  That wants to fly back to you.

THE KIND OLD MAN

THE kind old man—the mild old man—
  Who smiled on the boys at play,
Dreaming, perchance, of his own glad youth
  When he was as blithe and gay!

And the larger urchin tossed the ball,
  And the lesser held the bat—
Though the kindly old man's eyes were blurred
  He could even notice that!

But suddenly he was shocked to hear
  Words that I dare not write,
And he hastened, in his kindly way,
  To curb them as he might!

And he said, "Tut! tut! you naughty boy
  With the ball! for shame!" and then,
"You boy with the bat, whack him over the
      head
  If he calls you that again!"

The kind old man—the mild old man—
  Who gazed on the boys at play,
Dreaming, perchance, of his own wild youth
  When he was as tough as they!

A SCRAWL

I WANT to sing something—but this is all—
   I try and I try, but the rhymes are dull
As though they were damp, and the echoes fall
      Limp and unlovable.

Words will not say what I yearn to say—
   They will not walk as I want them to,
But they stumble and fall in the path of the way
      Of my telling my love for you.

Simply take what the scrawl is worth—
   Knowing I love you as sun the sod
On the ripening side of the great round earth
      That swings in the smile of God.

AWAY

I CAN not say, and I will not say
   That he is dead.—He is just away!

With a cheery smile, and a wave of the hand,
He has wandered into an unknown land,

And left us dreaming how very fair
It needs must be, since he lingers there.

And you—O you, who the wildest yearn
For the old-time step and the glad return,—

Think of him faring on, as dear
In the love of There as the love of Here;

And loyal still, as he gave the blows
Of his warrior-strength to his country's foes.—

Mild and gentle, as he was brave,—
When the sweetest love of his life he gave

To simple things:—Where the violets grew
Blue as the eyes they were likened to,

The touches of his hands have strayed
As reverently as his lips have prayed:

When the little brown thrush that harshly chirred
Was dear to him as the mocking-bird;

And he pitied as much as a man in pain
A writhing honey-bee wet with rain.—

Think of him still as the same, I say:
He is not dead—he is just away!

A MONUMENT FOR THE SOLDIERS

A MONUMENT for the Soldiers!
  And what will ye build it of?
Can ye buiid it of marble, or brass, or bronze,
  Outlasting the Soldiers' love?
Can ye glorify it with legends
  As grand as their blood hath writ
From the inmost shrine of this land of thine
  To the outermost verge of it?

And the answer came: We would build it
  Out of our hopes made sure,
And out of our purest prayers and tears,
  And out of our faith secure:
We would build it out of the great white truths
  Their death hath sanctified,
And the sculptured forms of the 'men in arms,
  And their faces ere they died.

And what heroic figures
  Can the sculptor carve in stone?
Can the marble breast be made to bleed,
  And the marble lips to moan?

Can the marble brow be fevered?
  And the marble eyes be graved
To look their last, as the flag floats past,
  On the country they have saved?

And the answer came: The figures
  Shall all be fair and brave,
And, as befitting, as pure and white
  As the stars above their grave!
The marble lips, and breast and brow
  Whereon the laurel lies,
Bequeath us right to guard the flight
  Of the old flag in the skies!

A monument for the Soldiers!
  Built of a people's love,
And blazoned and decked and panoplied
  With the hearts ye build it of!
And see that ye build it stately,
  In pillar and niche and gate,
And high in pose as the souls of those
  It would commemorate!

OUT TO OLD AUNT MARY'S

WASN'T it pleasant, O brother mine,
In those old days of the lost sunshine
Of youth—when the Saturday's chores were
through,
And the "Sunday's wood" in the kitchen, too,
And we went visiting, "me and you,"
Out to Old Aunt Mary's?—

"Me and you"—And the morning fair,
With the dewdrops twinkling everywhere;
The scent of the cherry-blossoms blown
After us, in the roadway lone,
Our capering shadows onward thrown—
Out to Old Aunt Mary's!

It all comes back so clear to-day!
Though I am as bald as you are gray,—
Out by the barn-lot and down the lane
We patter along in the dust again,
As light as the tips of the drops of the rain
Out to Old Aunt Mary's.

The few last houses of the town;
Then on, up the high creek-bluffs and down;
Past the squat toll-gate, with its well-sweep pole

"The Woodland echoes with yells of mirth"

The bridge, and "the old 'babtizin'-hole,' "
Loitering, awed, o'er pool and shoal,
   Out to Old Aunt Mary's.

We cross the pasture, and through the wood,
Where the old gray snag of the poplar stood,
   Where the hammering "red-heads" hopped awry,
   And the buzzard "raised" in the "clearing"-sky
   And lolled and circled, as we went by
      Out to Old Aunt Mary's.

Or, stayed by the glint of the redbird's wings,
Or the glitter of song that the bluebird sings,
   All hushed we feign to strike strange trails,
   As the "big braves" do in the Indian tales,
   Till again our real quest lags and fails—
      Out to Old Aunt Mary's.—

And the woodland echoes with yells of mirth
That make old war-whoops of minor worth! . . .
   Where such heroes of war as we?—
   With bows and arrows of fantasy,
   Chasing each other from tree to tree
      Out to Old Aunt Mary's!

And then in the dust of the road again;
And the teams we met, and the countrymen;
   And the long highway, with sunshine spread
   As thick as butter on country bread,
   Our cares behind, and our hearts ahead
      Out to Old Aunt Mary's.—

For only, now, at the road's next bend
To the right we could make out the gable-end
  Of the fine old Huston homestead—not
  Half a mile from the sacred spot
  Where dwelt our Saint in her simple cot—
      Out to Old Aunt Mary's.

Why, I see her now in the open door
Where the little gourds grew up the sides and o'er
  The clapboard roof!—And her face—ah, me!
  Wasn't it good for a boy to see—
  And wasn't it good for a boy to be
      Out to Old Aunt Mary's?—

The jelly—the jam and the marmalade,
And the cherry and quince "preserves" she made!
  And the sweet-sour pickles of peach and pear,
  With cinnamon in 'em, and all things rare!—
  And the more we ate was the more to spare,
      Out to Old Aunt Mary's!

Ah! was there, ever, so kind a face
And gentle as hers, or such a grace
  Of welcoming, as she cut the cake
  Or the juicy pies that she joyed to make
  Just for the visiting children's sake—
      Out to Old Aunt Mary's!

The honey, too, in its amber comb
One only finds in an old farm-home;
  And the coffee, fragrant and sweet, and ho!

So hot that we gloried to drink it so,
With spangles of tears in our eyes, you know—
    Out to Old Aunt Mary's.

And the romps we took, in our glad unrest !—
Was it the lawn that we loved the best,
    With its swooping swing in the locust trees,
    Or was it the grove, with its leafy breeze,
    Or the dim haymow, with its fragrancies—
        Out to Old Aunt Mary's.

Far fields, bottom-lands, creek-banks—all,
We ranged at will.—Where the waterfall
    Laughed all day as it slowly poured
    Over the dam by the old mill-ford,
    While the tail-race writhed, and the mill-wheel
        roared—
        Out to Old Aunt Mary's.

But home, with Aunty in nearer call,
That was the best place, after all !—
    The talks on the back porch, in the low
    Slanting sun and the evening glow,
    With the voice of counsel that touched us so,
        Out to Old Aunt Mary's.

And then, in the garden—near the side
Where the beehives were and the path was wide,—
    The apple-house—like a fairy cell—
    With the little square door we knew so well,
    And the wealth inside but our tongues could tell—
        Out to Old Aunt Mary's.

And the old spring-house, in the cool green gloom
Of the willow trees,—and the cooler room
   Where the swinging shelves and the crocks were
      kept,
   Where the cream in a golden languor slept,
   While the waters gurgled and laughed and
      wept—
        Out to Old Aunt Mary's.

And as many a time have you and I—
Barefoot boys in the days gone by—
   Knelt, and in tremulous ecstasies
   Dipped our lips into sweets like these,—
   Memory now is on her knees
        Out to Old Aunt Mary's.—

For, O my brother so far away,
This is to tell you—she waits *to-day*
   To welcome us:—Aunt Mary fell
   Asleep this morning, whispering, "Tell
   The boys to come." . . . And all is well
        Out to Old Aunt Mary's.

IN THE AFTERNOON

YOU in the hammock; and I, near by,
    Was trying to read, and to swing you, too;
And the green of the sward was so kind to the eye,
    And the shade of the maples so cool and blue,
    That often I looked from the book to you
To say as much, with a sigh.

You in the hammock. The book we'd brought
    From the parlor—to read in the open air,—
Something of love and of Launcelot
    And Guinevere, I believe, was there—
    But the afternoon, it was far more fair
Than the poem was, I thought.

You in the hammock; and on and on
    I droned and droned through the rhythmic stuff—
But, with always a half of my vision gone
    Over the top of the page—enough
    To caressingly gaze at you, swathed in the fluff
Of your hair and your odorous "lawn."

You in the hammock—and that was a year—
   Fully a year ago, I guess—
And what do we care for their Guinevere
   And her Launcelot and their lordliness!—
   You in the hammock still, and—Yes—
Kiss me again, my dear!

UNINTERPRETED

SUPINELY we lie in the grove's shady greenery,
  Gazing, all dreamy-eyed, up through the
      trees,—
And as to the sight is the heavenly scenery,
  So to the hearing the sigh of the breeze.

We catch but vague rifts of the blue through the
      wavering
  Boughs of the maples; and, like undefined,
The whispers and lisps of the leaves, faint and
      quavering,
  Meaningless falter and fall on the mind.

The vine, with its beauty of blossom, goes rioting
  Up by the casement, as sweet to the eye
As the trill of the robin is restful and quieting
  Heard in a drowse with the dawn in the sky.

And yet we yearn on to learn more of the mystery—
  We see and we hear, but forever remain
Mute, blind and deaf to the ultimate history
  Born of a rose or a patter of rain.

BILLY'S ALPHABETICAL ANIMAL SHOW

A WAS an elegant Ape
  Who tied up his ears with red tape,
     And wore a long veil
     Half revealing his tail
Which was trimmed with jet bugles and
     crape.

B was a boastful old Bear
  Who used to say,—"Hoomh! I declare
     I can eat—if you'll get me
     The children, and let me—
Ten babies, teeth, toe-nails and hair!"

C was a Codfish who sighed
  When snatched from the home of his
     pride,
     But could he, embrined,
     Guess this fragrance behind,
How glad he would be to have died!

D was a dandified Dog
  Who said,—"Though it's raining like
     fog
     I wear no umbrellah,
     Me boy, for a fellah
Might just as well travel incog!"

1012

E was an elderly Eel
   Who would say,—"Well, I really feel—
     As my grandchildren wriggle
     And shout 'I should giggle'—
A trifle run down at the heel!"

F was a Fowl who conceded
   Some hens might hatch more eggs than
     she did,—
     But she'd children as plenty
     As eighteen or twenty,
And that was quite all that she needed.

G was a gluttonous Goat
   Who, dining one day, *table d'hôte,*
     Ordered soup-bone, *au fait,*
     And fish, *papier-mâché,*
And a *filet* of Spring overcoat.

H was a high-cultured Hound
   Who could clear forty feet at a bound,
     And a coon once averred
     That his howl could be heard
For five miles and three-quarters around.

I was an Ibex ambitious
   To dive over chasms auspicious;
     He would leap down a peak
     And not light for a week,
And swear that the jump was delicious.

J was a Jackass who said
He had such a bad cold in his head,
    If it wasn't for leaving
    The rest of us grieving,
He'd really rather be dead.

K was a profligate Kite
Who would haunt the saloons every night;
    And often he ust
    To reel back to his roost
Too full to set up on it right.

L was a wary old Lynx
Who would say,—"Do you know wot I
      thinks?—
    I thinks ef you happen
    To ketch me a-nappin'
I'm ready to set up the drinks!"

M was a merry old Mole,
Who would snooze all day in his hole,
    Then—all night, a-rootin'
    Around and galootin'—
He'd sing "Johnny, Fill up the Bowl!"

N was a caustical Nautilus
Who sneered, "I suppose, when they've
      caught all us,
    Like oysters they'll serve us,
    And can us, preserve us,
And barrel, and pickle, and bottle us!"

O was an autocrat Owl—
    Such a wise—such a wonderful fowl!
      Why, for all the night through
      He would hoot and hoo-hoo,
And hoot and hoo-hooter and howl!

P was a Pelican pet,
    Who gobbled up all he could get;
      He could eat on until
      He was full to the bill,
And there he had lodgings to let!

Q was a querulous Quail,
    Who said: "It will little avail
      The efforts of those
      Of my foes who propose
To attempt to put salt on my tail!"

R was a ring-tailed Raccoon,
    With eyes of the tinge of the moon,
      And his nose a blue-black,
      And the fur on his back
A sad sort of sallow maroon.

S is a Sculpin—you'll wish
    Very much to have one on your dish,
      Since all his bones grow
      On the outside, and so
He's a very desirable fish.

T was a Turtle, of wealth,
    Who went round with particular stealth,
        "Why," said he, "I'm afraid
        Of being waylaid
When I even walk out for my health!"

U was a Unicorn curious,
    With one horn, of a growth so *luxurious,*
        He could level and stab it—
        If you didn't grab it—
Clean through you, he was so blamed
        furious!

V was a vagabond Vulture
    Who said: "I don't want to insult yer,
        But when you intrude
        Where in lone solitude
I'm a-preyin', you're no man o' culture!"

W was a wild *Wood*chuck,
    And you just bet that he *could* "chuck"—
        He'd eat raw potatoes,
        Green corn, and tomatoes,
And tree roots, and call it all *"good* chuck!"

X was a kind of X-cuse
    Of some-sort-o'-thing that got loose
        Before we could name it,
        And cage it, and tame it,
And bring it in general use.

Y is a Yellowbird,—bright
  As a petrified lump of starlight,
    Or a handful of lightning-
    Bugs, squeezed in the tight'ning
Pink fist of a boy, at night.

Z is the Zebra, of course!—
  A kind of a clown-of-a-horse,—
    Each other despising,
    Yet neither devising
A way to obtain a divorce!

& here is the famous—what-is-it?
  Walk up, Master Billy, and quiz it:
    You've seen the *rest* of 'em—
    Ain't this the *best* of 'em,
Right at the end of your visit?

THE PIXY PEOPLE

IT was just a very
    Merry fairy dream!—
All the woods were airy
    With the gloom and gleam;
Crickets in the clover
    Clattered clear and strong,
And the bees droned over
    Their old honey-song!

In the mossy passes,
    Saucy grasshoppers
Leaped about the grasses
    And the thistle-burs;
And the whispered chuckle
    Of the katydid
Shook the honeysuckle-
    Blossoms where he hid.

Through the breezy mazes
    Of the lazy June,
Drowsy with the hazes
    Of the dreamy noon,

1018

Little Pixy people
  Winged above the walk,
Pouring from the steeple
  Of a mullein-stalk.

One—a gallant fellow—
  Evidently King,—
Wore a plume of yellow
  In a jeweled ring
On a pansy bonnet,
  Gold and white and blue,
With the dew still on it,
  And the fragrance, too.

One—a dainty lady,—
  Evidently Queen—
Wore a gown of shady
  Moonshine and green,
With a lace of gleaming
  Starlight that sent
All the dewdrops dreaming
  Everywhere she went.

One wore a waistcoat
  Of rose-leaves, out and in;
And one wore a faced-coat
  Of tiger-lily-skin;
And one wore a neat coat
  Of palest galingale;
And one a tiny street-coat,
  And one a swallow-tail.

And Ho! sang the King of them,
　And Hey! sang the Queen;
And round and round the ring of them
　Went dancing o'er the green;
And Hey! sang the Queen of them,
　And Ho! sang the King—
And all that I had seen of them
　—Wasn't anything!

It was just a very
　Merry fairy dream!—
All the woods were airy
　With the gloom and gleam;
Crickets in the clover
　Clattered clear and strong,
And the bees droned over
　Their old honey-song!

THE TOWN KARNTEEL

THE town Karnteel!—It's who'll reveal
   Its praises jushtifiable?
For who can sing av anything
   So lovely and reliable?
Whin Summer, Spring, or Winter lies
   From Malin's Head to Tipperary,
There's no such town for interprise
   Bechuxt Youghal and Londonderry!

There's not its likes in Ireland—
   For twic't the week, be-gorries!
They're playing jigs upon the band,
And joomping there in sacks—and—and—
   And racing, wid wheelborries!

Karnteel—it's there, like any fair,
   The purty gurrls is plinty, sure!—
And, man-alive! at forty-five
   The legs av me air twinty, sure!
I lave me cares, and hoein', too,
   Behint me, as is sinsible,
And it's Karnteel I'm goin' to,
   To cilebrate in principle!

For there's the town av all the land!
  And twic't the week, be-gorries!
They're playing jigs upon the band,
And joomping there in sacks—and—and—
  And racing, wid wheelborries!

And whilst I feel for owld Karnteel
  That I've no phrases glorious,
It stands above the need av love
  That boasts in voice uproarious!—
Lave that for Cork, and Dublin, too,
  And Armagh and Killarney, thin,—
And Karnteel won't be troublin' you
  Wid any jilous blarney, thin!

For there's the town av all the land!
  Where twic't the week, be-gorries!
They're playing jigs upon the band,
And joomping there in sacks—and—and—
  And racing, wid wheelborries!

DONN PIATT OF MAC-O-CHEE

I

DONN PIATT—of Mac-o-chee,—
   Not the one of History,
Who, with flaming tongue and pen,
Scathes the vanities of men;
Not the one whose biting wit
Cuts pretense and etches it
On the brazen brow that dares
Filch the laurel that it wears:
Not the Donn Piatt whose praise
Echoes in the noisy ways
Of the faction, onward led
By the statesman!—But, instead,
Give the simple man to me,—
Donn Piatt of Mac-o-chee!

II

Donn Piatt of Mac-o-chee!
Branches of the old oak tree,
Drape him royally in fine
Purple shade and golden shine!
Emerald plush of sloping lawn
Be the throne he sits upon!
And, O Summer Sunset, thou

Be his crown, and gild a brow
Softly smoothed and soothed and calmed
By the breezes, mellow-palmed
As Erata's white hand agleam
On the forehead of a dream.—
So forever rule o'er me,
Donn Piatt of Mac-o-chee!

III

Donn Piatt of Mac-o-chee!
Through a lilied memory
Plays the wayward little creek
Round thy home at hide-and-seek—
As I see and hear it, still
Romping round the wooded hill,
Till its laugh and babble blends
With the silence while it sends
Glances back to kiss the sight,
In its babyish delight,
Ere it strays amid the gloom
Of the glens that burst in bloom
Of the rarest rhyme for thee,
Donn Piatt of Mac-o-chee!

IV

Donn Piatt of Mac-o-chee!
What a darling destiny
Has been mine—to meet him there—
Lolling in an easy chair

On the terrace, while he told
Reminiscences of old—
Letting my cigar die out,
Hearing poems talked about;
And entranced to hear him say
Gentle things of Thackeray,
Dickens, Hawthorne, and the rest,
Known to him as host and guest—
Known to him as he to me—
Donn Piatt of Mac-o-chee!

HERR WEISER

HERR WEISER!—Threescore years and
ten,—
A hale white rose of his countrymen,
Transplanted here in the Hoosier loam,
And blossomy as his German home—
As blossomy and as pure and sweet
As the cool green glen of his calm retreat,
Far withdrawn from the noisy town
Where trade goes clamoring up and down.
Whose fret and fever, and stress and strife,
May not trouble his tranquil life!

Breath of rest, what a balmy gust!—
Quit of the city's heat and dust,
Jostling down by the winding road,
Through the orchard ways of his quaint abode.—
Tether the horse, as we onward fare
Under the pear trees trailing there,
And thumping the wooden bridge at night
With lumps of ripeness and lush delight,
Till the stream, as it maunders on till dawn,
Is powdered and pelted and smiled upon.

Herr Weiser, with his wholesome face,
And the gentle blue of his eyes, and grace
Of unassuming honesty,
Be there to welcome you and me!
And what though the toil of the farm be stopped
And the tireless plans of the place be dropped,
While the prayerful master's knees are set
In beds of pansy and mignonette
And lily and aster and columbine,
Offered in love, as yours and mine?—

What, but a blessing of kindly thought,
Sweet as the breath of forget-me-not!—
What, but a spirit of lustrous love
White as the aster he bends above!—
What, but an odorous memory
Of the dear old man, made known to me
In days demanding a help like his,—
As sweet as the life of the lily is—
As sweet as the soul of a babe, bloom-wise
Born of a lily in Paradise.

FROM DELPHI TO CAMDEN

I

FROM Delphi to Camden—little Hoosier
    towns,—
But here were classic meadows, blooming dales and
    downs;
And here were grassy pastures, dewy as the leas
Trampled over by the trains of royal pageantries!

And here the winding highway loitered through the
    shade
Of the hazel covert, where, in ambuscade,
Loomed the larch and linden, and the greenwood-
    tree
Under which bold Robin Hood loud hallooed to me!

Here the stir and riot of the busy day
Dwindled to the quiet of the breath of May;
Gurgling brooks, and ridges lily-marged and
    spanned
By the rustic bridges found in Wonderland!

II

From Delphi to Camden,—from Camden back
    again!—
And now the night was on us, and the lightning and
    the rain;
And still the way was wondrous with the flash of
    hill and plain,—
The stars like printed asterisks—the moon a murky
    stain!

And I thought of tragic idyl, and of flight and hot
    pursuit,
And the jingle of the bridle and cuirass and spur on
    boot,
As our horses' hooves struck showers from the
    flinty boulders set
In freshet-ways of writhing reed and drowning
    violet.

And we passed beleaguered castles, with their
    battlements a-frown;
Where a tree fell in the forest was a turret toppled
    down;
While my master and commander—the brave knight
    I galloped with
On this reckless road to ruin or to fame was—Dr.
    Smith!

A NOON INTERVAL

A DEEP, delicious hush in earth and sky—
 A gracious lull—since, from its wakening,
 The morn has been a feverish, restless thing
In which the pulse of Summer ran too high
And riotous, as though its heart went nigh
 To bursting with delights past uttering:
 Now, as an o'erjoyed child may cease to sing
All falteringly at play, with drowsy eye
 Draining the pictures of a fairy tale
To brim his dreams with—there comes o'er the day
 A loathful silence, wherein all sounds fail
Like loitering tones of some faint roundelay . . .
 No wakeful effort longer may avail—
The wand waves, and the dozer sinks away.

AT MADAME MANICURE'S

DAINTIEST of Manicures!
   What a cunning hand is yours;
And how awkward, rude and great
Mine, as you manipulate!
Wonderfully cool and calm
Are the touches of your palm
To my fingers, as they rest
In their rosy, cozy nest,
While your own, with deftest skill,
Dance and caper as they will,—
Armed with instruments that seem
Gathered from some fairy dream—
Tiny spears, and simitars
Such as pixy armorers
Might have made for jocund fays
To parade on holidays,
And flash round in dewy dells,
Lopping down the lily-bells;
Or in tilting, o'er the leas,
At the clumsy bumblebees,
Splintering their stings, perchance,
As the knights in old romance
Snapped the spears of foes that fought

In the jousts at Camelot!
Smiling? Dainty Manicure?—
'Twould delight me, but that you're
Simply smiling, as I see,
At my nails and not at me!
Haply this is why they glow
And light up and twinkle so!

JOHN McKEEN

JOHN McKEEN, in his rusty dress,
  His loosened collar, and swarthy throat,
His face unshaven, and none the less,
His hearty laugh and his wholesomeness,
  And the wealth of a workman's vote!

Bring him, O Memory, here once more,
  And tilt him back in his Windsor chair
By the kitchen stove, when the day is o'er
And the light of the hearth is across the floor,
  And the crickets everywhere!

And let their voices be gladly blent
  With a watery jingle of pans and spoons,
And a motherly chirrup of sweet content,
And neighborly gossip and merriment,
  And old-time fiddle-tunes!

Tick the clock with a wooden sound,
  And fill the hearing with childish glee
Of rhyming riddle, or story found
In the Robinson Crusoe, leather-bound
  Old book of the Used-to-be!

John McKeen of the Past! Ah, John,
    To have grown ambitious in worldly ways!—
To have rolled your shirt-sleeves down, to don
A broadcloth suit, and, forgetful, gone
    Out on election days!

John, ah, John! did it prove your worth
    To yield you the office you still maintain?—
To fill your pockets, but leave the dearth
Of all the happier things on earth
    To the hunger of heart and brain?

Under the dusk of your villa trees,
    Edging the drives where your blooded span
Paw the pebbles and wait your ease,—
Where are the children about your knees,
    And the mirth, and the happy man?

The blinds of your mansion are battened to;
    Your faded wife is a close recluse;
And your "finished" daughters will doubtless do
Dutifully all that is willed of you,
    And marry as you shall choose!—

But O for the old-home voices, blent
    With the watery jingle of pans and spoons,
And the motherly chirrup of glad content,
And neighborly gossip and merriment,
    And the old-time fiddle-tunes!

THE BOY-FRIEND

CLARENCE, my boy-friend, hale and strong!
O he is as jolly as he is young;
And all of the laughs of the lyre belong
    To the boy all unsung:

So I want to sing something in his behalf—
    To clang some chords, for the good it is
To know he is near, and to have the laugh
    Of that wholesome voice of his.

I want to tell him in gentler ways
    Than prose may do, that the arms of rhyme,
Warm and tender with tuneful praise,
    Are about him all the time.

I want him to know that the quietest nights
    We have passed together are yet with me,
Roistering over the old delights
    That were born of his company.

I want him to know how my soul esteems
    The fairy stories of Andersen,
And the glad translations of all the themes
    Of the hearts of boyish men.

Want him to know that my fancy flows,
    With the lilt of a dear old-fashioned tune,
Through "Lewis Carroll's" poemly prose,
    And the tale of "The Bold Dragoon."

O this is the Prince that I would sing—
    Would drape and garnish in velvet line,
Since courtlier far than any king
    Is this brave boy-friend of mine.

WHEN BESSIE DIED

"If from your own the dimpled hands had slipped,
And ne'er would nestle in your palm again;
If the white feet into the grave had tripped"——

WHEN Bessie died—
    We braided the brown hair, and tied
It just as her own little hands
Had fastened back the silken strands
A thousand times—the crimson bit
Of ribbon woven into it
That she had worn with childish pride—
Smoothed down the dainty bow—and cried—
                When Bessie died.

When Bessie died—
We drew the nursery blinds aside,
And, as the morning in the room
Burst like a primrose into bloom,
Her pet canary's cage we hung
Where she might hear him when he sung—
And yet not any note he tried
Though she lay listening folded-eyed.

When Bessie died—
We writhed in prayer unsatisfied:
We begged of God, and He did smile
In silence on us all the while;
And we did see Him, through our tears,
Enfolding that fair form of hers,
She laughing back against His love
The kisses we had nothing of—
And death to us He still denied,
When Bessie died—
                    When Bessie died.

THE RIVALS; OR THE SHOWMAN'S RUSE

A TRAGI-COMEDY, IN ONE ACT

PERSONS REPRESENTED

BILLY MILLER   }
JOHNNY WILLIAMS }   The Rivals
TOMMY WELLS   Conspirator

TIME—Noon. SCENE—Country Town—*Rear view of the* Miller Mansion, *showing Barn, with practical loft-window opening on alley-way, with colored-crayon poster on wall beneath, announcing:*—"BILLY MILLER's Big Show and Monstur Circus and Equareum! A shour-bath fer Each and All fer 20 pins. This Afternoon! Don't fer git the Date!" *Enter* TOMMY WELLS *and* JOHNNY WILLIAMS, *who gaze a while at poster,* TOMMY *secretly smiling and winking at* BILLY MILLER, *concealed at loft-window above.*

TOMMY [*To* JOHNNY]

Guess 'at Billy hain't got back,—
Can't see nothin' through the crack—
Can't hear nothin' neether—No!
. . . Thinks he's got the dandy show,
Don't he?

1039

JOHNNY [*Scornfully*]

'Course! but what *I* care?—
He hain't got no show in there!—
What's *he* got in there but that
Old hen, cooped up with a cat
An' a turkle, an' that thing
'At he calls his "circus-ring"?
What a "circus-ring"! I'd *quit!*
Bet *mine's* twic't as big as it!

TOMMY

Yes, but *you* got no machine
W'at you bathe with, painted green,
With a string to work it, guess!

JOHNNY [*Contemptuously*]

Folks don't *bathe* in *circuses!*—
Ladies comes to *mine,* you bet!
I' got seats where *girls* can set;
An' a dressin'-room, an' all,
Fixed up in my pony's stall—
Yes, an' I got *carpet,* too,
Fer the tumblers, an' a blue
Center-pole!

TOMMY

Well, Billy, he's
Got a tight-rope an' trapeze,

An' a hoop 'at he jumps through
Head-first!

JOHNNY

Well, what's *that* to do—
Lightin' on a pile o' hay?
Hain't no *actin'* thataway!

TOMMY

Don't care what you say, he draws
Bigger crowds than you do, 'cause
Sence he started up, I know
All the fellers says his show
Is the best-un!

JOHNNY

Yes, an' he
Better not tell things on me!
His old circus hain't no good!—
'Cause he's got the neighborhood
Down on me he thinks 'at I'm
Goin' to stand it all the time;
Thinks ist 'cause my Pa don't 'low
Me to fight, he's got me now,
An' can say I lie, an' call
Me ist anything at all!
Billy Miller thinks I am
'Feard to say 'at he says *"dam"*—
Yes, an' *worser* ones! an' I'm

Goin' to tell his folks sometime!—
An' ef he don't shet his head
I'll tell worse 'an *that* he said
When he fighted Willie King—
An' got licked like ever'thing!—
Billy Miller better shin
Down his Daddy's lane ag'in,
Like a cowardy-calf, an' climb
In fer home another time!
Better—

[*Here* BILLY *leaps down from the loft upon his un-
suspecting victim; and two minutes later,*
JOHNNY, *with the half of a straw hat, a bleeding nose, and a straight rent across one trou-
sers-knee, makes his inglorious—exit.*]

THE CHRIST

"FATHER!" (so The Word) He cried,—
    "Son of Thine, and yet denied;
By my brothers dragged and tried,
Scoffed and scourged, and crucified,
With a thief on either side—
Brothers mine, alike belied,—
Arms of mercy open wide,
Father! Father!" So He died.

TO HEAR HER SING

To hear her sing—to hear her sing—
It is to hear the birds of Spring
In dewy groves on blooming sprays
Pour out their blithest roundelays.

It is to hear the robin trill
At morning, or the whippoorwill
At dusk, when stars are blossoming—
To hear her sing—to hear her sing!

To hear her sing—it is to hear
The laugh of childhood ringing clear
In woody path or grassy lane
Our feet may never fare again.

Faint, far away as Memory dwells,
It is to hear the village bells
At twilight, as the truant hears
Them, hastening home, with smiles and tears.

Such joy it is to hear her sing,
We fall in love with everything—
The simple things of every day
Grow lovelier than words can say.

The idle brooks that purl across
The gleaming pebbles and the moss
We love no less than classic streams—
The Rhines and Arnos of our dreams.

To hear her sing—with folded eyes,
It is, beneath Venetian skies,
To hear the gondoliers' refrain,
Or troubadours of sunny Spain.—

To hear the bulbul's voice that shook
The throat that trilled for Lalla Rookh:
What wonder we in homage bring
Our hearts to her—to hear her sing!

FROM THE HEADBOARD OF A GRAVE
IN PARAGUAY

A TROTH, and a grief, and a blessing,
Disguised them and came this way,—
And one was a promise, and one was a doubt,
And one was a rainy day.

And they met betimes with this maiden,—
And the promise it spake and lied,
And the doubt it gibbered and hugged itself,
And the rainy day—she died.

A CANARY AT THE FARM

FOLKS has be'n to town, and Sahry
   Fetched 'er home a pet canary,—
And of all the blame', contrary,
     Aggervatin' things alive!
I love music—that's I love it
When it's *free*—and plenty of it;—
But I kind o' git above it,
     At a dollar-eighty-five!

Reason's plain as I'm a-sayin',—
Jes' the idy, now, o' layin'
Out yer money, and a-payin'
     Fer a willer-cage and bird,
When the medder-larks is wingin'
Round you, and the woods is ringin'
With the beautifullest singin'
     That a mortal ever heard!

Sahry's sot, tho'.—So I tell her
He's a purty little feller,
With his wings o' creamy-yeller
     And his eyes keen as a cat.

And the twitter o' the critter
'Pears to absolutely glitter!
Guess I'll haf to go and git her
    A high-priceter cage 'n that!

SEPTEMBER DARK

I

THE air falls chill;
   The whippoorwill
Pipes lonesomely behind the hill:
The dusk grows dense,
The silence tense;
And, lo, the katydids commence.

II

Through shadowy rifts
Of woodland, lifts
The low, slow moon, and upward drifts,
While left and right
The fireflies' light
Swirls eddying in the skirts of Night.

III

O Cloudland, gray
And level, lay
Thy mists across the face of Day!
At foot and head,
Above the dead,
O Dews, weep on uncomforted!

ANSELMO

YEARS did I vainly seek the good Lord's
    grace.—
  Prayed, fasted, and did penance dire and dread;
Did kneel, with bleeding knees and rainy face,
  And mouth the dust, with ashes on my head;
Yea, still with knotted scourge the flesh I flayed,
  Rent fresh the wounds, and moaned and shrieked
    insanely;
And froth oozed with the pleadings that I made,
  And yet I prayed on vainly, vainly, vainly!

A time, from out of swoon I lifted eye,
  To find a wretched outcast, gray and grim,
Bathing my brow, with many a pitying sigh,
  And I did pray God's grace might rest on him.—
Then, lo! a gentle voice fell on mine ears—
  "Thou shalt not sob in suppliance hereafter;
Take up thy prayers and wring them dry of tears,
  And lift them, white and pure with love and
    laughter!"

    So is it now for all men else I pray;
    So is it I am blest and glad alway.

1050

TIME OF CLEARER TWITTERINGS

I

TIME of crisp and tawny leaves,
    And of tarnished harvest sheaves,
And of dusty grasses—weeds—
Thistles, with their tufted seeds
Voyaging the Autumn breeze
Like as fairy argosies:
Time of quicker flash of wings,
And of clearer twitterings
In the grove or deeper shade
Of the tangled everglade,—
Where the spotted water-snake
Coils him in the sunniest brake;
And the bittern, as in fright,
Darts, in sudden, slanting flight,
Southward, while the startled crane
Films his eyes in dreams again.

II

Down along the dwindled creek
We go loitering. We speak
Only with old questionings
Of the dear remembered things

Of the days of long ago,
When the stream seemed thus and so
In our boyish eyes:—The bank
Greener then, through rank on rank
Of the mottled sycamores,
Touching tops across the shores:
Here, the hazel thicket stood—
There, the almost pathless wood
Where the shellbark hickory tree
Rained its wealth on you and me.
Autumn! as you loved us then,
Take us to your heart again!

III

Season halest of the year!
How the zestful atmosphere
Nettles blood and brain and smites
Into life the old delights
We have wasted in our youth,
And our graver years, forsooth!
How again the boyish heart
Leaps to see the chipmunk start
From the brush and sleek the sun's
Very beauty, as he runs!
How again a subtle hint
Of crushed pennyroyal or mint
Sends us on our knees, as when
We were truant boys of ten—
Brown marauders of the wood,
Merrier than Robin Hood!

IV

Ah! will any minstrel say,
In his sweetest roundelay,
What is sweeter, after all,
Than black haws, in early Fall?—
Fruit so sweet the frost first sat,
Dainty-toothed, and nibbled at!
And will any poet sing
Of a lusher, richer thing
Than a ripe May-apple, rolled
Like a pulpy lump of gold
Under thumb and finger-tips,
And poured molten through the lips?
Go, ye bards of classic themes,
Pipe your songs by classic streams!
I would twang the redbird's wings
In the thicket while he sings!

THE BOYS

WHERE are they?—the friends of my child-
       hood enchanted—
The clear, laughing eyes looking back in my own,
And the warm, chubby fingers my palms have so
    wanted,
    As when we raced over
          Pink pastures of clover,
And mocked the quail's whir and the bumblebee's
    drone?

Have the breezes of time blown their blossomy faces.
    Forever adrift down the years that are flown?
Am I never to see them romp back to their places,
    Where over the meadow,
          In sunshine and shadow,
The meadow-larks trill, and the bumblebees drone?

Where are they? Ah! dim in the dust lies the clover;
    The whippoorwill's call has a sorrowful tone,
And the dove's—I have wept at it over and over;—
    I want the glad luster
          Of youth, and the cluster
Of faces asleep where the bumblebees drone!

LINCOLN

A PEACEFUL life;—just toil and rest—
All his desire;—
To read the books he liked the best
Beside the cabin fire—
God's word and man's;—to peer sometimes
Above the page, in smoldering gleams,
And catch, like far heroic rhymes,
The on-march of his dreams.

A peaceful life;—to hear the low
Of pastured herds,
Or woodman's ax that, blow on blow,
Fell sweet as rhythmic words.
And yet there stirred within his breast
A fateful pulse that, like a roll
Of drums, made high above his rest
A tumult in his soul.

A peaceful life! . . . They haled him even
As One was haled
Whose open palms were nailed toward Heaven
When prayers nor aught availed.

And, lo, he paid the selfsame price
To lull a nation's awful strife
And will us, through the sacrifice
Of self, his peaceful life.

THE BLIND GIRL

IF I might see his face to-day!—
  He is so happy now!—To hear
His laugh is like a roundelay—
  So ringing-sweet and clear!
His step—I heard it long before
He bounded through the open door
To tell his marriage.—Ah! so kind—
So good he is!—And I—so blind!

But thus he always came to me—
  Me, first of all, he used to bring
His sorrow to—his ecstasy—
  His hopes and everything;
And if I joyed with him or wept,
It was not long *the music* slept,—
And if he sung, or if I played—
Or both,—we were the braver made.

I grew to know and understand
  His every word at every call,—
The gate-latch hinted, and his hand
  In mine confessed it all:

He need not speak one word to me—
He need not sigh—I need not see,—
But just the one touch of his palm,
And I would answer—song or psalm.

He wanted recognition—name—
  He hungered so for higher things,—
The altitudes of power and fame,
  And all that fortune brings:
Till, with his great heart fevered thus,
And aching as impetuous,
I almost wished sometimes that *he*
Were blind and patient made, like me.

But he has won!—I knew he would.—
  Once in the mighty Eastern mart,
I knew his music only could
  Be sung in every heart!
And when he proudly sent me **this**
From out the great metropolis,
I bent above the graven score
And, weeping, kissed it o'er and o'er.—

And yet not blither sing the birds
  Than this glad melody,—the tune
As sweetly wedded with the words
  As flowers with middle-June;
Had he not *told* me, I had known
It was composed of love alone—
His love for *her.*—And she can see
His happy face eternally!—

While *I*—O God, forgive, I pray!—
  Forgive me that I did so long
To look upon his face to-day!—
  I know the wish was wrong.—
Yea, I am thankful that my sight
Is shielded safe from such delight:—
I can pray better, with this blur
Of blindness—both for him and her.

THE KING

THEY rode right out of the morning sun—
  A glimmering, glittering cavalcade
Of knights and ladies, and every one
    In princely sheen arrayed;
And the king of them all, O he rode ahead,
With a helmet of gold, and a plume of red
That spurted about in the breeze and bled
    In the bloom of the everglade.

And they rode high over the dewy lawn,
  With brave, glad banners of every hue
That rolled in ripples, as they rode on
    In splendor, two and two;
And the tinkling links of the golden reins
Of the steeds they rode rang such refrains
As the castanets in a dream of Spain's
    Intensest gold and blue.

And they rode and rode; and the steeds they neighed
  And pranced, and the sun on their glossy hides
Flickered and lightened and glanced and played
    Like the moon on rippling tides;

And their manes were silken, and thick and
    strong,
And their tails were flossy, and fetlock-long,
And jostled in time to the teeming throng,
      And their knightly song besides.

Clank of scabbard and jingle of spur,
  And the fluttering sash of the queen went wild
In the wind, and the proud king glanced at her
      As one at a wilful child,—
And as knight and lady away they flew,
And the banners flapped, and the falcon, too,
And the lances flashed and the bugle blew,
      He kissed his hand and smiled.—

And then, like a slanting sunlit shower,
  The pageant glittered across the plain,
And the turf spun back, and the wild-weed flower
      Was only a crimson stain.
And a dreamer's eyes they are downward cast,
As he blends these words with the wailing blast:
"It is the King of the Year rides past!"
      And Autumn is here again.

A LIZ-TOWN HUMORIST

SETTIN' round the stove, last night,
Down at Wess's store, was me
And Mart Strimples, Tunk, and White,
And Doc Bills, and two er three
Fellers o' the Mudsock tribe
No use tryin' to describe!
And says Doc, he says, says he,—
"Talkin' 'bout good things to eat,
Ripe mushmillon's hard to beat!"

I chawed on. And Mart he 'lowed
Wortermillon beat the mush.—
"Red," he says, "and juicy—Hush!—
I'll jes' leave it to the crowd!"
Then a Mudsock chap, says he,—
"Punkin's good enough fer me—
Punkin pies, I mean," he says,—
"Them beats millons!—What say, Wess?"

I chawed on. And Wess says,—"Well,
You jes' fetch that wife of mine
All yer wortermillon-*rine*,—
And she'll bile it down a spell—

In with sorghum, I suppose,
And what else, Lord only knows!—
But I'm here to tell all hands
Them p'serves meets my demands!"

I chawed on. And White he says,—
"Well, I'll jes' stand in with Wess—
I'm no hog!" And Tunk says,—"I
Guess I'll pastur' out on pie
With the Mudsock boys!" says he;
"Now what's yourn?" he says to me:
I chawed on—fer—quite a spell—
Then I speaks up, slow and dry,—
"Jes' tobacker!" I-says-I.—
And you'd ort o' heerd 'em yell!

LIKE HIS MOTHER USED TO MAKE

"Uncle Jake's Place," St. Jo, Missouri, 1874.

"I WAS born in Indiany," says a stranger, lank
    and slim,
As us fellers in the restarunt was kind o' guyin'
    him,
And Uncle Jake was slidin' him another punkin pie
And a' extry cup o' coffee, with a twinkle in his
    eye,—
"I was born in Indiany—more'n forty year' ago—
And I hain't be'n back in twenty—and I'm workin'
    back'ards slow;
But I've et in ever' restarunt 'twixt here and Santy
    Fee,
And I want to state this coffee tastes like gittin'
    home, to me!

"Pour us out another, Daddy," says the feller,
    warmin' up,
A-speakin' 'crost a saucerful, as Uncle tuk his cup,—
"When I seed yer sign out yander," he went on, to
    Uncle Jake,—
" 'Come in and git some coffee like yer mother used
    to make'—

I thought of *my* old mother, and the Posey County
    farm,
And me a little kid ag'in, a-hangin' in her arm,
As she set the pot a-bilin', broke the eggs and
    poured 'em in"—
And the feller kind o' halted, with a trimble in his
    chin:

And Uncle Jake he fetched the feller's coffee back,
    and stood
As solemn, fer a minute, as a' undertaker would;
Then he sort o' turned and tiptoed to'rds the kitchen
    door—and nex',
Here comes his old wife out with him, a-rubbin' of
    her specs—
And she rushes fer the stranger, and she hollers out,
    "It's him!—
Thank God we've met him comin'!—Don't you
    know yer mother, Jim?"
And the feller, as he grabbed her, says,—"You bet I
    hain't forgot—
But," wipin' of his eyes, says he, "yer coffee's
    mighty hot!"

A GOLDEN WEDDING

DECEMBER—1884

YOUR Golden Wedding!—fifty years
   Of comradeship, through smiles and tears!
Through summer sun, and winter sleet,
You walked the ways with willing feet;
For, journeying together thus,
Each path held something glorious.
No winter wind could blow so chill
But found you even warmer still
In fervor of affection—blest
In knowing all was for the best;
And so, content, you faced the storm
And fared on, smiling, arm in arm.

But why this moralizing strain
Beside a hearth that glows again
As on your *Wooden* wedding-day?—
When butter-prints and paddles lay
Around in dough-bowls, tubs and churns,
And all such "woodenish" concerns;
And "woodenish" they are—for now
Who can afford to keep a cow

And pestle some old churn, when you
Can buy good butter—"golden," too—
Far cheaper than you can afford
To make it and neglect the Lord!

And round your hearth the faces gleam
That may recall, as in a dream,
The brightness of a time when *Tin*
Came glittering and clanging in
And raising noise enough to seize
And settle any swarm of bees!
But those were darling times, no doubt,—
To see the mother pouring out
The "tins" of milk, and tilting up
The coffee-pot above each cup;
Or, with the ladle from the wall,
Dipping and serving mush for all.

And *all* the "weddings," as they came,—
The *"Glass,"* the *"China,"*—still the same
You see them, till the last ere this,—
The *"Silver,"*—and your wedded bliss
Abated not!—for love appears
Just silvered over with the years:—
Silver the grandchild's laugh you hear—
Silver his hopes, and silver-clear
Your every prayer for him,—and still
Silver your hope, through good and ill—
Silver and silver everywhere,
Bright as the silver of your hair!

But on your *Golden* Wedding!—Nay—
What can I give to you to-day
Who am too very poor indeed
To offer what I so much need?
If gold I gave, I fear, alack!
I'd needs provide you gave it back,
To stay me, the long years before
I'd stacked and heaped five dollars more!
And so, in lieu—and little worse—
I proffer you this dross of verse—
The merest tinsel, I admit,—
But take it—I have more of it.

HIS CHRISTMAS SLED

I

I WATCH him with his Christmas sled;
  He hitches on behind
A passing sleigh, with glad hooray,
  And whistles down the wind;
He hears the horses champ their bits,
  And bells that jingle-jingle—
You Woolly Cap! you Scarlet Mitts!
  You miniature "Kriss Kringle"!

I almost catch your secret joy—
  Your chucklings of delight,
The while you whiz where glory is
  Eternally in sight!
With you I catch my breath, as swift
  Your jaunty sled goes gliding
O'er glassy track and shallow drift,
  As I behind were riding!

II

He winks at twinklings of the frost,
  And on his airy race,
Its tingles beat to redder heat
  The rapture of his face:—

The colder, keener is the air,
  The less he cares a feather.
But, there! he's gone! and I gaze on
  The wintriest of weather!

Ah, Boy! still speeding o'er the track
  Where none returns again,
To sigh for you, or cry for you,
  Or die for you were vain.—
And so, speed on! the while I pray
  All nipping frosts forsake you—
Ride still ahead of grief, but may
  All glad things overtake you!

A NEW YEAR'S TIME AT WILLARDS'S

I

THE HIRED MAN TALKS

THERE'S old man Willards; an' his wife;
 An' Marg'et—S'repty's sister;—an'
There's me—an' I'm the hired man;
An' Tomps McClure, you bet yer life!

Well, now, old Willards hain't so bad,
Considerin' the chance he's had.
Of course, he's rich, an' sleeps an' eats
 Whenever he's a mind to: Takes
An' leans back in the Amen-seats
 An' thanks the Lord fer all he makes.—
That's purty much all folks has got
Ag'inst the old man, like as not!
But there's his woman—jes' the turn
Of them-air two wild girls o' hern—
 Marg'et an' S'repty—allus in
Fer any cuttin'-up concern—
 Church festibals, an' foolishin'

Round Christmas-trees, an' New Year's sprees—
  Set up to watch the Old Year go
An' New Year come—sich things as these;
  An' turkey-dinners, don't you know!
S'repty's younger, an' more gay,
  An' purtier, an' finer dressed
  Than Marg'et is—but, lawsy-day!
  She hain't the independentest!—
"Take care!" old Willards used to say,
"Take care!—Let Marg'et have her way,
An' S'repty, you go off an' play
On your melodeum!"—But, best
  Of all, comes Tomps! An' I'll be bound,
Ef he hain't jes' the beatin'est
  Young chap in all the country round!
    Ef you know Tomps you'd like him, shore!
  They hain't no man on top o' ground
    Walks into my affections more!—
An' all the Settlement'll say
That Tomps was liked jes' thataway
  By ever'body, till he tuk
    A shine to S'repty Willards.—Then
You'd ort 'o see the old man buck
An' h'ist hisse'f, an' paw the dirt,
    An' hint that "common workin'-men
That didn't want their feelin's hurt
    'Ud better hunt fer 'comp'ny' where
    The folks was pore an' didn't care!"—
The pine-blank facts is,—the old man,
  Last Christmas was a year ago,

Well, blame-don! ef I ever see
  Sich impidence! I couldn't say
Not nary word! But Mother she
  Sot out a cheer fer Tomps, an' they
Shuk hands an' turnt their back on me.
Then I riz—mad as mad could be!—
  But Marg'et says,—"Now, Pap! you set
  Right where you're settin'!—Don't you fret!
An', Tomps—*you* warm yer feet!" says she,
  "An' throw yer mitts an' comfert on
  The bed there! Where is S'repty gone?—
  The cabbage is a-scortchin'! Ma,
  Stop cryin' there an' stir the slaw!"
Well!—what was *Mother cryin'* fer?—
  I half riz up—but Marg'et's chin
  Hit squared—an' I set down ag'in—
I allus *was* afeard o' her,
I was, by jucks! So there I set,
Betwixt a sinkin'-chill an' sweat,
An' scuffled with my wrath, an' shet
My teeth to mighty tight, you bet!
  An' yit, fer all that I could do,
I *eeched* to jes' git up an' whet
  The carvin'-knife a rasp er two
  On Tomps's ribs—an' so would you!—
Fer he had riz an' faced around,
  An' stood there, smilin', as they brung
The turkey in, all stuffed an' browned—
  Too sweet fer nose er tooth er tongue!
    With sniffs o' sage, an' p'r'aps a dash

D—15

Of old burnt brandy, steamin'-hot,
　Mixed kind o' in with apple-mash
　An' mince-meat, an' the Lord knows what!
Nobody was a-talkin' then,
　To 'filiate my awk'ardness—
　No noise o' any kind but jes'
The rattle o' the dishes when
They'd fetch 'em in an' set 'em down,
An' fix an' change 'em round an' round,
　Like women does—till Mother says,—
"Vittels is ready; Abner, call
　Down S'repty—she's up-stairs, I guess."—
And Marg'et *she* says, "Ef you bawl
Like that, she'll not come down at all!
Besides, we needn't wait till *she*
Gits down! Here, Tomps, set down by me,
　An' Pap: say grace!" . . . Well, there I was!—
What *could* I do! I drapped my head
Behind my fists an' groaned, an' said:—

　"Indulgent Parent! in Thy cause
　　We bow the head an' bend the knee,
An' break the bread, an' pour the wine,
　　Feelin' "—(The stair-door suddenly
　Went bang! an' S'repty flounced by me)—
"Feelin'," I says, "this feast is Thine—
　This New Year's feast"—an' *rap-rap-rap!*
　Went Marg'et's case-knife on her plate—
An' next, I heerd a sasser drap,—
　Then I looked up, an', strange to state,
There S'repty set in Tomps's lap—
　An' huggin' him, as shore as fate!

An' Mother kissin' him k-slap!—
An' Marg'et—she chips in to drap
  The ruther peert remark to me:—
  "That 'grace' o' yourn," she says, "won't 'gee'—
This hain't no *'New Year's* feast,'" says she,—
"This is a' INFAIR-Dinner, Pap!"

An' so it was!—be'n married fer
Purt' nigh a week!—'Twas Marg'et planned
    The whole thing fer 'em, through an'
      through
  I'm rickonciled; an', understand,
I take things jes' as they occur,—
    Ef *Marg'et* liked Tomps, Tomps 'ud do!—
But I-says-I, a-holt his hand,—
"I'm glad you didn't marry HER—
'Cause *Marg'et's* my *guardeen*—yes-*sir!*—
  An' S'repty's good enough fer you!"

WHATEVER THE WEATHER MAY BE

"WHATEVER the weather may be," says
  he—
  "Whatever the weather may be,
It's plaze, if ye will, an' I'll say me say,—
Supposin' to-day was the winterest day,
Wud the weather be changing because ye cried,
Or the snow be grass were ye crucified?
The best is to make yer own summer," says he,
"Whatever the weather may be," says he—
  "Whatever the weather may be!

"Whatever the weather may be," says he—
  "Whatever the weather may be,
It's the songs ye sing, an' the smiles ye wear,
That's a-makin' the sun shine everywhere;
An' the world of gloom is a world of glee,
Wid the bird in the bush, an' the bud in the tree,
An' the fruit on the stim o' the bough," says he,
"Whatever the weather may be," says he—
  "Whatever the weather may be!

"Whatever the weather may be," says he—
  "Whatever the weather may be,
Ye can bring the Spring, wid its green an' gold,
An' the grass in the grove where the snow lies cold;
An' ye'll warm yer back, wid a smiling face,
As ye sit at yer heart, like an owld fireplace,
An' toast the toes o' yer sowl," says he,
"Whatever the weather may be," says he—
  "Whatever the weather may be!"

A LEAVE-TAKING

SHE will not smile;
  She will not stir;
I marvel while
  I look on her.
    The lips are chilly
      And will not speak;
    The ghost of a lily
      In either cheek.

Her hair—ah me!
  Her hair—her hair!
How helplessly
  My hands go there!
    But my caresses
      Meet not hers,
    O golden tresses
      That thread my tears?

I kiss the eyes
  On either lid,
Where her love lies
  Forever hid.
    I cease my weeping
      And smile and say:
    I will be sleeping
      Thus, some day!

DOWN ON WRIGGLE CRICK

Best time to kill a hog's when he's fat
—OLD SAW

MOSTLY, folks is law-abidin'
   Down on Wriggle Crick,—
Seein' they's no Squire residin'
   In our bailywick;
No grand juries, no suppeenies,
   Ner no vested rights to pick
Out yer man, jerk up and jail ef
   He's outragin' Wriggle Crick!

Wriggle Crick hain't got no lawin',
   Ner no suits to beat;
Ner no court-house gee-and-hawin'
   Like a County-seat;
Hain't no waitin' round fer verdicks,
   Ner non-gittin' witness-fees;
Ner no thiefs 'at gits "new hearin's,"
   By some lawyer slick as grease!

Wriggle Crick's leadin' spirit
   Is old Johnts Culwell,—
Keeps post-office, and right near it
   Owns what's called "The Grand Hotel"—

(Warehouse now)—buys wheat and ships it;
  Gits out ties, and trades in stock,
And knows all the high-toned drummers
  'Twixt South Bend and Mishawauk.

Last year comes along a feller—
  Sharper 'an a lance—
Stovepipe-hat and silk umbreller,
  And a boughten all-wool pants,—
Tinkerin' of clocks and watches;
  Says a trial's all he wants—
And rents out the tavern-office
  Next to Uncle Johnts.

Well.—He tacked up his k'dentials,
  And got down to biz.—
Captured Johnts by cuttin' stenchils
  Fer them old wheat-sacks o' his.—
Fixed his clock, in the post-office—
  Painted fer him, clean and slick,
'Crost his safe, in gold-leaf letters,
  "J. Culwells's, Wriggle Crick."

Any kind o' job you keered to
  Resk him with, and bring,
He'd fix fer you—jes' appeared to
  Turn his hand to anything!—
Rings, er earbobs, er umbrellers—
  Glue a cheer er chany doll,—
W'y, of all the beatin' fellers,
  He jes' beat 'em all!

Made his friends, but wouldn't stop there,—
  One mistake he learnt,
That was, sleepin' in his shop there.—
  And one Sund'y night it burnt!
Come in one o' jes' a-sweepin'
  All the whole town high and dry—
And that feller, when they waked him,
  Suffocatin', mighty nigh!

Johnts he drug him from the buildin',
  He'pless—*'peared* to be,—
And the women and the childern
  Drenchin' him with sympathy!
But I noticed Johnts helt on him
  With a' extry lovin' grip,
And the men-folks gathered round him
  In most warmest pardnership!

That's the whole mess, grease-and-dopin'!
  Johnts's safe was saved,—
But the lock was found sprung open,
  And the inside caved.
Was no trial—ner no jury—
  Ner no jedge ner court-house-click.—
Circumstances alters cases
  Down on Wriggle Crick!

LORD BACON

WRITTEN AS A JOKE AND ASCRIBED TO A VERY PRAC-
TICAL BUSINESS MAN, AMOS J. WALKER

MASTER of masters in the days of yore,
  When art met insult, with no law's redress;
When Law itself insulted Righteousness,
And Ignorance thine own scholastic lore,
And thou thine own judicial office more,—
  What master living now canst love thee less,
  Seeing thou didst thy greatest art repress
And leave the years its riches to restore
To us, thy long neglectors. Yield us grace
  To make becoming recompense, and dawn
On us thy poet-smile; nor let us trace,
  In fancy, where the old-world myths have gone,
The shade of Shakespeare, with averted face,
  Withdrawn to uttermost oblivion.

MY FIRST WOMERN

I BURIED my first womern
    In the spring; and in the fall
I was married to my second,
    And hain't settled yit at all!—
Fer I'm allus thinkin'—thinkin'
    Of the first one's peaceful ways,
A-bilin' soap and singin'
    Of the Lord's amazin' grace.

And I'm thinkin' of her, constant,
    Dyin' carpet-chain and stuff,
And a-makin' up rag carpets,
    When the *floor* was good enough!
And I mind her he'p a-feedin'
    And I riccollect her now
A-drappin' corn, and keepin'
    Clos't behind me and the plow!

And I'm allus thinkin' of her
    Reddin' up around the house;
Er cookin' fer the farm-hands;
    Er a-drivin' up the cows.—

And there she lays out yander
  By the lower medder fence,
Where the cows was barely grazin',
  And they're usin' ever sence.

And when I look acrost there—
  Say it's when the clover's ripe,
And I'm settin', in the evenin',
  On the porch here, with my pipe,
And the *other'n* hollers "Henry!"—
  W'y they ain't no sadder thing
Than to think of my first womern
  And her funeral last spring
    Was a year ago—

THE QUEST

I AM looking for Love. Has he passed this way,
  With eyes as blue as the skies of May,
And a face as fair as the summer dawn?—
You answer back, but I wander on,—
For you say: "Oh, yes; but his eyes were gray,
And his face as dim as a rainy day."

Good friends, I query, I search for Love;
His eyes are as blue as the skies above,
And his smile as bright as the midst of May
When the truce-bird pipes: Has he passed this way?
And one says: "Ay; but his face, alack!
Frowned as he passed, and his eyes were black."

O who will tell me of Love? I cry!
His eyes are as blue as the mid-May sky,
And his face as bright as the morning sun;
And you answer and mock me, every one,
That his eyes were dark, and his face was wan,
And he passed you frowning and wandered on.

But stout of heart will I onward fare,
Knowing *my* Love is beyond—somewhere,—
The Love I seek, with the eyes of blue,
And the bright, sweet smile unknown of you;
And on from the hour his trail is found
I shall sing sonnets the whole year round.

TO AN IMPORTUNATE GHOST

GET gone, thou most uncomfortable ghost!
Thou really dost annoy me with thy thin
Impalpable transparency of grin;
And the vague, shadowy shape of thee almost
Hath vexed me beyond boundary and coast
Of my broad patience. Stay thy chattering chin,
And reel the tauntings of thy vain tongue in,
Nor tempt me further with thy vaporish boast
That I am *helpless* to combat thee! Well,
Have at thee, then! Yet if a doom most dire
Thou wouldst escape, flee whilst thou canst!—
Revile
Me not, Miasmic Mist!—Rank Air! *Retire!*
One instant longer an thou haunt'st me, I'll
Inhale thee, O thou wraith despicable!

WHO BIDES HIS TIME

WHO bides his time, and day by day
    Faces defeat full patiently,
And lifts a mirthful roundelay,
    However poor his fortunes be,—
He will not fail in any qualm
    Of poverty—the paltry dime
It will grow golden in his palm,
        Who bides his time.

Who bides his time—he tastes the sweet
    Of honey in the saltest tear;
And though he fares with slowest feet,
    Joy runs to meet him, drawing near:
The birds are heralds of his cause;
    And, like a never-ending rhyme,
The roadsides bloom in his applause,
        Who bides his time.

Who bides his time, and fevers not
    In the hot race that none achieves,
Shall wear cool-wreathen laurel, wrought
    With crimson berries in the leaves;

1089

And he shall reign a goodly king,
   And sway his hand o'er every clime,
With peace writ on his signet-ring,
   Who bides his time.

AS WE READ BURNS

WHO is speaking? Who has spoken?
  Whose voice ceasing thus has broken
The sweet pathos of our dreams?
Sweetest bard of sweetest themes,
  Pouring in each poet-heart
  Some rare essence of your art
  Till it seems your singing lip
  Kisses every pencil tip!
Far across the unknown lands—
  Reach of heavenly isle and sea—
How we long to touch the hands
  You outhold so lovingly!

WHEN JUNE IS HERE

WHEN June is here—what art have we to sing
   The whiteness of the lilies 'midst the green
Of noon-tranced lawns? or flash of roses seen
Like redbirds' wings? or earliest ripening
Prince-harvest apples, where the cloyed bees cling
   Round winy juices oozing down between
   The peckings of the robin, while we lean
In under-grasses, lost in marveling;
   Or the cool term of morning, and the stir
Of odorous breaths from wood and meadow walks;
   The Bob-white's liquid yodel, and the whir
Of sudden flight; and, where the milkmaid talks
Across the bars, on tilted barley-stalks
   The dewdrops' glint in webs of gossamer.

AT NOON—AND MIDNIGHT

FAR in the night, and yet no rest for him! The
　　pillow next his own
The wife's sweet face in slumber pressed—yet he
　　awake—alone! alone!
In vain he courted sleep;—one thought would ever
　　in his heart arise,—
The harsh words that at noon had brought the tear-
　　drops to her eyes.

Slowly on lifted arm he raised and listened. All was
　　still as death;
He touched her forehead as he gazed, and listened
　　yet, with bated breath:
Still silently, as though he prayed, his lips moved
　　lightly as she slept—
For God was with him, and he laid his face with
　　hers and wept.

TO JAMES NEWTON MATTHEWS

IN ANSWER TO A LETTER ON THE ANATOMY OF THE
SONNET

OHO! ye sunny, sonnet-singin' vagrant,
   Flauntin' your simmer sangs in sic a weather!
Ane maist can straik the bluebells and the heather
Keekin' aboon the snaw and bloomin' fragrant!
Whiles you, ye whustlin' brither, sic a lay grant
   O' a' these janglin', wranglin' sweets thegither,
  I weel maun perk my ain doon-drappin' feather
And pipe a wee: Tho' boisterous and flagrant
The winds blow whuzzle-whazzle rhymes that trickle
   Fra' aff my tongue less limpid than I'd ha'e them,
I in their little music hap a mickle
   O' canty praises, a' asklent to weigh them
Agen your pride, and smile to see them tickle
  The warm nest o' the heart wherein I lay them.

SPIRITS AT HOME

THE FAMILY

THERE was Father, and Mother, and Emmy,
    and Jane,
  And Lou, and Ellen, and John and me—
And Father was killed in the war, and Lou
She died of consumption, and John did too,
  And Emmy she went with the pleurisy.

THE SPIRITS

Father believed in 'em all his life—
  But Mother, at first, she'd shake her head—
Till after the battle of Champion Hill,
When many a flag in the winder-sill
  Had crape mixed in with the white and red!

I used to doubt 'em myself till then—
  But me and Mother was satisfied
When Ellen she set, and Father came
And rapped "God Bless You!" and Mother's name,
  And "The Flag's up here!" . . . And we all just
    cried.

Used to come often, after that,
　And talk to us—just as he used to do,
Pleasantest kind! And once, for John,
He said he was "lonesome, but wouldn't let on—
　Fear Mother would worry, and Emmy and Lou."

But Lou was the bravest girl on earth—
　For all she never was hale and strong,
She'd have her fun!—With her voice clean lost
She'd laugh and joke us that "when *she* crossed
　To Father, *we'd* all come taggin' along!"

Died—just that way! And the raps was thick
　That night, as they often since occur,
Extry loud! And when *Lou* got back
She said it was Father and her—and *"whack!"*
　She tuk the table—and we knowed *her!*

John and Emmy, in five years more,
　Both had went.—And it seemed like fate,—
For the old home *it* burnt down.—But Jane
And me and Ellen we built again
　The new house, here, on the old estate.

And a happier family I don't know
　*Of any*wheres—unless it's *them,*—
Father, with all his love for Lou,
And her there with him, and healthy, too,
　And laughin', with John and little Em.

And, first we moved in the *new* house here,
  They all dropped in for a long powwow:—
"We like your buildin', of course," Lou said,—
"But wouldn't swap with you to save your head—
  For *we* live in the ghost of the old house now!"

ART AND LOVE

HE faced his canvas (as a seer whose ken
 Pierces the crust of this existence through)
 And smiled beyond on that his genius knew
Ere mated with his being. Conscious then
Of his high theme alone, he smiled again
 Straight back upon himself in many a hue
 And tint, and light and shade, which slowly grew
Enfeatured of a fair girl's face, as when
 First time she smiles for love's sake with no fear.
So wrought he, witless that behind him leant
 A woman, with old features, dim and sear,
 And glamoured eyes that felt the brimming tear,
And with a voice, like some sad instrument,
 That sighing said, "I'm dead there; love me
  here!"

SONG

O I would I had a lover!
  A lover! a lover!
O I would I had a lover
  With a twinkering guitar,
    To come beneath my casement
Singing "There is none above her,"
While I, leaning, seemed to hover
  In the scent of his cigar!

Then at morn I'd want to meet him—
  To meet him! to meet him!
O at morn I'd want to meet him,
  When the mist was in the sky,
    And the dew along the path I went
To casually greet him,
And to cavalierly treat him,
  And regret it by and by.

And I'd want to meet his brother—
  His brother! his brother!
O I'd want to meet his brother
  At the german or the play,

To pin a rose on his lapel
And lightly press the other,
And love him like a mother—
    While he thought the other way.

O I'd pitilessly test him!
    And test him! and test him!
O I'd pitilessly test him
    Far beyond his own control;
        And every tantalizing lure
With which I could arrest him,
I'd loosen to molest him,
    Till I tried his very soul.

But ah, when I relented!
    Relented, relented!
But ah, when I relented—
    When the stars were blurred and dim,
        And the moon above, with crescent grace,
Looked off as I repented,
And with rapture half demented,
    All my heart went out to him!

PAP'S OLD SAYIN'

PAP had one old-fashioned sayin'
    That I'll never quite fergit—
And they's seven growed-up childern
    Of us rickollects it yit!—
Settin' round the dinner-table,
    Talkin' 'bout our friends, perhaps,
Er abusin' of our neghbors,
    I kin hear them words o' Pap's—
        "Shet up, and eat yer vittels!"

Pap he'd never argy with us,
    Ner cut any subject short
Whilse we all kep' clear o' gossip,
    And wuz actin' as we ort:
But ef we'd git out o' order—
    Like sometimes a fambly is,—
Faultin' folks, er one another,
    Then we'd hear that voice o' his—
        "Shet up, and eat yer vittels!"

Wuz no hand hisse'f at talkin'—
    Never hadn't *much* to say,—
Only, as I said, pervidin'
    When we'd rile him thataway:

1101

Then he'd allus lose his temper
   Spite o' fate, and jerk his head
And slam down his case-knife vicious'
   Whilse he glared around and said—
     "Shet up, and eat yer vittels!"

Mind last time 'at Pap was ailin'
   With a misery in his side,
And had hobbled in the kitchen—
   Jes' the day before he died,—
Laury Jane she ups and tells him,
   "Pap, you're pale as pale kin be—
Hain't ye 'feard them-air cowcumbers
   Hain't good fer ye?" And says he,
     "Shet up, and eat yer vittels!"

Well! I've saw a-many a sorrow,—
   Forty year', through thick and thin;
I've got best,—and I've got *worsted,*
   Time and time and time ag'in!—
But I've met a-many a trouble
   That I hain't run on to twice,
Haltin'-like and thinkin' over
   Them-air words o' Pap's advice:
     "Shet up, and eat yer vittels!"

GRANNY

GRANNY'S come to our house,
And ho! my lawzy-daisy!
All the childern round the place
Is ist a-runnin' crazy!
Fetched a cake fer little Jake,
And fetched a pie fer Nanny,
And fetched a pear fer all the pack
That runs to kiss their Granny!

Lucy Ellen's in her lap,
And Wade and Silas Walker
Both's a-ridin' on her foot,
And 'Pollos on the rocker;
And Marthy's twins, from Aunt Marinn's,
And little Orphant Annie,
All's a-eatin' gingerbread
And giggle-un at Granny!

Tells us all the fairy tales
Ever thought er wundered—
And 'bundance o' other stories—
Bet she knows a hunderd!—

Bob's the one fer "Whittington,"
  And "Golden Locks" fer Fanny!
Hear 'em laugh and clap their hands,
  Listenin' at Granny!

"Jack the Giant-Killer" 's good;
  And "Bean-Stalk" 's another!—
So's the one of "Cinderell' "
  And her old godmother;—
That-un's best of all the rest—
  Bestest one of any,—
Where the mices scampers home
  Like we runs to Granny!

Granny's come to our house,
  Ho! my lawzy-daisy!
All the childern round the place
  Is ist a-runnin' crazy!
Fetched a cake fer little Jake,
  And fetched a pie fer Nanny,
And fetched a pear fer all the pack
  That runs to kiss their Granny!

BECALMED

I

WOULD that the winds might only blow
  As they blew in the golden long ago!—
Laden with odors of Orient isles
Where ever and ever the sunshine smiles,
And the bright sands blend with the shady trees,
And the lotus blooms in the midst of these.

II

Warm winds won from the midland vales
To where the tress of the Siren trails
O'er the flossy tip of the mountain phlox
And the bare limbs twined in the crested rocks,
High above as the sea-gulls flap
Their lopping wings at the thunderclap.

III

Ah! that the winds might rise and blow
The great surge up from the port below,
Bloating the sad, lank, silken sails
Of the Argo out with the swift, sweet gales

That blew from Colchis when Jason had
His love's full will and his heart was glad—
When Medea's voice was soft and low.
Ah! that the winds might rise and blow!

GRIGGSBY'S STATION

PAP'S got his pattent-right, and rich as all crea-
        tion;
    But where's the peace and comfort that we all had
        before?
Le's go a-visitin' back to Griggsby's Station—
    Back where we ust to be so happy and so pore!

The likes of us a-livin' here! It's jes' a mortal pity
    To see us in this great big house, with cyarpets on
        the stairs,
And the pump right in the kitchen! And the city!
    city! city!—
    And nothin' but the city all around us ever'-
        wheres!

Climb clean above the roof and look from the
        steeple,
    And never see a robin, nor a beech or ellum tree!
And right here in ear-shot of at least a thousan'
        people,
    And none that neighbors with us or we want to
        go and see!

Le's go a-visitin' back to Griggsby's Station—
    Back where the latch-string's a-hangin' from the
        door,
And ever' neighbor round the place is dear as a re-
        lation—
    Back where we ust to be so happy and so pore!

I want to see the Wiggenses, the whole kit-and-
        bilin',
    A-driven' up from Shallor Ford to stay the Sun-
        day through;
And I want to see 'em hitchin' at their son-in-law's
        and pilin'
    Out there at 'Lizy Ellen's like they ust to do!

I want to see the piece-quilts the Jones girls is
        makin';
    And I want to pester Laury 'bout their freckled
        hired hand,
And joke her 'bout the widower she come purt' nigh
        a-takin',
    Till her Pap got his pension 'lowed in time to save
        his land.

Le's go a-visitin' back to Griggsby's Station—
    Back where they's nothin' aggervatin' any more,
Shet away safe in the woods around the old
        location—
    Back where we ust to be so happy and so pore!

I want to see Marindy and he'p her with her sewin',
    And hear her talk so lovin' of her man that's dead
      and gone,
And stand up with Emanuel to show me how he's
    growin',
    And smile as I have saw her 'fore she putt her
      mournin' on.

And I want to see the Samples, on the old lower
    eighty,
    Where John, our oldest boy, he was tuk and
      burried—for
His own sake and Katy's,—and I want to cry with
    Katy
    As she reads all his letters over, writ from The
      War.

What's in all this grand life and high situation,
    And nary pink nor hollyhawk a-bloomin' at the
      door?—
Le's go a-visitin' back to Griggsby's Station—
    Back where we ust to be so happy and so pore!

FESSLER'S BEES

"TALKIN' 'bout yer bees," says Ike,
   Speakin' slow and ser'ous-like,
"D' ever tell you 'bout old 'Bee'—
Old 'Bee' Fessler?" Ike says-he!
"Might call him a *bee-expert,*
When it come to handlin' bees,—
Roll the sleeves up of his shirt
And wade in amongst the trees
Where a swarm 'u'd settle, and—
Blam'dest man on top of dirt!—
Rake 'em with his naked hand
Right back in the hive ag'in,
Jes' as easy as you please!
Nary bee 'at split the breeze
Ever jabbed a stinger in
Old 'Bee' Fessler—jes' in fun,
Er in *airnest*—nary one!—
Couldn't agg one *on* to, nuther,
Ary one way er the other!

"Old 'Bee' Fessler," Ike says-he,
"Made a speshyality
Jes' o' bees; and built a shed—
Len'th about a half a mild!
Had about a *thousan'* head

O' hives, I reckon—tame and wild!
Durndest buzzin' ever wuz—
Wuss'n telegraph-poles does
When they're sockin' home the news
Tight as they kin let 'er loose!
Visitors rag out and come
Clean from town to hear 'em hum,
And stop at the kivered bridge;
But wuz some 'u'd cross the ridge
Allus, and go clos'ter—so 's
They could *see* 'em hum, I s'pose!
'Peared-like strangers down that track
Allus met folks comin' back
Lookin' extry fat and hearty
Fer a city picnic party!

"'Fore he went to Floridy,
Old 'Bee' Fessler," Ike says-he—
"Old 'Bee' Fessler couldn't bide
Childern on his place," says Ike.
"Yit, fer all, they'd climb inside
And tromp round there, keerless-like,
In their bare feet. 'Bee' could tell
Ev'ry town-boy by his yell—
So 's 'at when they bounced the fence,
Didn't make no difference!
He'd jes' git down on one knee
In the grass and pat the bee!—
And, ef 't 'adn't stayed stuck in,
Fess' 'u'd set the sting ag'in,
'N' potter off, and wait around

Fer the old famillyer sound.
Allus boys there, more or less,
Scootin' round the premises!
When the buckwheat wuz in bloom,
Lawzy! how them bees 'u'd boom
Round the boys 'at crossed that way
Fer the crick on Saturday!
Never seemed to me su'prisin'
'At the sting o' bees 'uz p'izin!

"'Fore he went to Floridy,"
Ike says, "nothin' 'bout a bee
'At old Fessler didn't know,—
W'y, it jes' 'peared-like 'at he
Knowed their language, high and low:
Claimed he told jes' by their buzz
What their wants and wishes wuz!
Peek in them-air little holes
Round the porches o' the hive—
Drat their pesky little souls!—
Could 'a' skinned the man alive!
Bore right in there with his thumb,
And squat down and scrape the gum
Outen ev'ry hole, and blow
'N' bresh the crumbs off, don't you know!
Take the roof off, and slide back
Them-air glass concerns they pack
Full o' honey, and jes' lean
'N' grabble 'mongst 'em fer the queen!
Fetch her out and *show* you to her—
Jes', you might say, *interview* her!

"Year er two," says Ike, says-he,
"'Fore he went to Floridy,
Fessler struck the theory,
Honey was the same as *love*—
You could make it day and night:
Said them bees o' his could be
Got jes' twic't the work out of
Ef a feller managed right.
He contended ef bees found
Blossoms all the year around,
He could git 'em down at once
To work all the *winter* months
Same as *summer*. So, one fall,
When their summer's work wuz done,
'Bee' turns in and robs 'em all;
Loads the hives then, one by one,
On the cyars, and 'lowed he'd see
Ef bees loafed in *Floridy!*
Said he bet he'd know the reason
Ef *his* didn't work that season!

"And," says Ike, "it's jes'," says-he,
"Like old Fessler says to me:
'Any man kin fool a *bee,*
Git him down in Floridy!'
'Peared at fust, as old 'Bee' said,
Fer to kind o' turn their head
Fer a spell; but, bless you! they
Didn't lose a half a day
Altogether!—Jes' lit in
Them-air tropics. and them-air

Cacktusses a-ripen-nin',
'N' magnolyers, and sweet peas,
'N' 'simmon and pineapple trees,
'N' ripe bananers, here and there,
'N' dates a-danglin' in the breeze,
'N' figs and reezins ev'rywhere,
All waitin' jes' fer Fessler's bees!
 N' Fessler's bees, with gaumy wings,
A-gittin' down and *whoopin'* things!—
Fessler kind o' overseein'
'Em, and sort o' *'hee-o-heein'!'*

"'Fore he went to *Floridy,*
Old 'Bee' Fessler," Ike says-he,
"Wuzn't counted, jes' to say,
Mean er or'n'ry anyway;
On'y ev'ry 'tarnel dime
'At 'u'd pass him on the road
He'd ketch up with, ev'ry time;
And no mortal ever knowed
Him to spend a copper cent—
'Less on some fool-*'speriment*
With them *bees*—like that-un he
Played on 'em in Floridy.
Fess', of course, *he* tuck his ease,
But 'twus *bilious* on the bees!
Sweat, you know, 'u'd jes' stand out
On their *forreds*—pant and groan,
And grunt round and limp about!—
And old 'Bee,' o' course, a-knowin'
'Twuzn't no fair shake to play

On them pore dumb insecks, ner
To abuse 'em thataway.
Bees has rights, I'm here to say,
And that's all they ast him fer!
Man as mean as *that,* jes' 'pears,
Could 'a' worked bees on the sheers!
Cleared big money—well, I guess,
'Bee' shipped honey, more er less,
Into ev'ry state, perhaps,
Ever putt down in the maps!

"But by time he fetched 'em back
In the spring ag'in," says Ike,
"They wuz actin' s'picious-like:
Though they 'peared to lost the track
O' ev'rything they saw er heard,
They'd lay round the porch, and gap'
At their shadders in the sun,
Do-less like, ontel some bird
Suddently 'u'd maybe drap
In a bloomin' churry tree,
Twitterin' a tune 'at run
In their minds familiously!
They'd revive up, kind o', then,
Like they argied: 'Well, it's be'n
The most longest summer we
Ever saw er want to see!
Must be *right,* though, er *old 'Bee'*
'U'd notify us!' they says-ee;
And they'd sort o' square their chin
And git down to work ag'in—

Moanin' round their honey-makin',
Kind o' like their head was achin'.
Tetchin' fer to see how they
Trusted Fessler thataway—
Him a-lazin' round, and smirkin'
To hisse'f to see 'em workin'!

"But old 'Bee,'" says Ike, says-he,—
"*Now* where is he? *Where's* he gone?
Where's the head he helt so free?
Where's his pride and vanity?
What's his hopes a-restin' on?—
Never knowed a man," says Ike,
"Take advantage of a bee,
'At affliction didn't strike
Round in that vicinity!
Sinners allus suffers some,
And *old Fessler's* reck'nin' come!
That-air man to-day is jes'
Like the grass 'at Scriptur' says
Cometh up, and then turns in
And jes' gits cut down ag'in!
Old 'Bee' Fessler," Ike says-he,
"Says, last fall, says he to me—
'Ike,' says he, 'them bees has jes'
Ciphered out my or'n'riness!
Nary bee in ary swarm
On the whole endurin' farm
Won't have nothin' more to do
With a man as mean as I've
Be'n to them, last year er two!

Nary bee in ary hive
But'll turn his face away,
Like they ort, whenever they
Hear my footprints drawin' nigh!'
And old 'Bee,' he'd sort o' shy
Round oneasy in his cheer,
Wipe his eyes, and yit the sap,
Spite o' all, 'u'd haf' to drap,
As he wound up: 'Wouldn't keer
Quite so much ef they'd jes' light
In and settle things up right,
Like they ort; but—blame the thing!—
'Pears-like they won't even *sting!*
Pepper me, the way I felt,
And I'd thank 'em, ev'ry welt!'
And as miz'able and mean
As 'Bee' looked, ef you'd 'a' seen
Them-air hungry eyes," says Ike,
"You'd fergive him, more'n like.

"Wisht you had 'a' knowed old 'Bee'
'Fore he went to Floridy!"

JONEY

HAD a harelip—Joney had:
  Spiled his looks, and Joney knowed it:
Fellers tried to bore him, bad—
But ef ever he got mad,
  He kep' still and never showed it.
'Druther have his mouth, all pouted
  And split up, and like it wuz,
Than the ones 'at laughed about it.—
  Purty is as purty does!

Had to listen ruther clos't
  'Fore you knowed what he wuz givin'
You; and yet, without no boast,
Joney he wuz jes' the most
  Entertainin' talker livin'!
Take the Scriptur's and run through 'em,
  Might say, like a' auctioneer,
And 'ud argy and review 'em
  'At wuz beautiful to hear!

Harelip and inpediment,
  Both wuz bad, and both ag'in' him—
But the *old folks* where he went,
'Peared like, knowin' his intent,
  'Scused his mouth fer what wuz in him.

And *the childern* all loved Joney—
  And he loved 'em back, you bet!—
Putt their arms around him——on'y
  None 'had ever kissed him yet!

In young company, someway,
  Boys 'ud grin at one another
On the sly; and girls 'ud lay
Low, with nothin' much to say,
  Er leave Joney with their mother.
Many and many a time he's fetched 'em
  Candy by the paper-sack,
And turned right around and ketched 'em
  Makin' mouths behind his back!

S'prised, sometimes, the slurs he took.—
  Chap said onc't his mouth looked sorter
Like a fish's mouth 'ud look
When he'd be'n jerked off the hook
  And plunked back into the worter.—
Same durn feller—it's su'prisin',
  But it's facts—'at stood and cherred
From the bank that big babtizin'
  'Pike-bridge accident occurred!—

Cherred fer Joney while he give
  Life to little childern drowndin'!
Which wuz fittenest to live—
Him 'at cherred, er him 'at div'
  And saved thirteen lives? . . . They found one

Body, three days later, floated
  Down the by-o, eight mile' south,
All so colored-up and bloated—
  On'y knowed him by his mouth!

Had a harelip—Joney had—
  Folks 'at filed apast all knowed it.—
Them 'at ust to smile looked sad,
But ef *he* thought good er bad,
  He kep' still and never showed it.
'Druther have that mouth, all pouted
  And split up, and like it wuz,
Than the ones 'at laughed about it.—
  Purty is as purty does!

KNEE-DEEP IN JUNE

I

TELL you what I like the best—
    'Long about knee-deep in June,
    'Bout the time strawberries melts
On the vine,—some afternoon
Like to jes' git out and rest,
    And not work at nothin' else!

II

Orchard's where I'd ruther be—
Needn't fence it in fer me!—
    Jes' the whole sky overhead,
And the whole airth underneath—
Sort o' so's a man kin breathe
    Like he ort, and kind o' has
Elbow-room to keerlessly
    Sprawl out len'thways on the grass
        Where the shadders thick and soft
    As the kivvers on the bed
        Mother fixes in the loft
Allus, when they's company!

III

Jes' a-sort o' lazin' there—
 S'lazy, 'at you peek and peer
  Through the wavin' leaves above,
  Like a feller 'ats in love
And don't know it, ner don't keer!
Ever'thing you hear and see
  Got some sort o' interest—
  Maybe find a bluebird's nest
Tucked up there conveenently
Fer the boy 'at's ap' to be
Up some other apple tree!
Watch the swallers skootin' past
Bout as peert as you could ast;
  Er the Bob-white raise and whiz
  Where some other's whistle is.

IV

Ketch a shadder down below,
And look up to find the crow—
Er a hawk,—away up there,
'Pearantly *froze* in the air!—
  Hear the old hen squawk, and squat
  Over ever' chick she's got,
Suddent-like!—and she knows where
  That-air hawk is, well as you!—
  You jes' bet yer life she do!—
   Eyes a-glitterin' like glass,
   Waitin' till he makes a pass!

V

Pee-wees' singin', to express
　My opinion, 's second-class,
Yit you'll hear 'em more er less;
　Sapsucks gittin' down to biz,
Weedin' out the lonesomeness;
　Mr. Bluejay, full o' sass,
　　In them baseball clothes o' his,
Sportin' round the orchard jes'
Like he owned the premises!
　Sun out in the fields kin sizz,
But flat on yer back, I guess,
　In the shade's where glory is!
That's jes' what I'd like to do
Stiddy fer a year er two!

VI

Plague! ef they ain't somepin' in
Work 'at kind o' goes ag'in'
　My convictions!—'long about
　　Here in June especially!—
　　Under some old apple tree,
　　　Jes' a-restin' through and through,
　I could git along without
　　　Nothin' else at all to do
　　　Only jes' a-wishin' you
Wuz a-gittin' there like me,
And June wuz eternity!

VII

Lay out there and try to see
Jes' how lazy you kin be!—
    Tumble round and souse yer head
In the clover-bloom, er pull
      Yer straw hat acrost yer eyes
       And peek through it at the skies,
    Thinkin' of old chums 'at's dead,
      Maybe, smilin' back at you
In betwixt the beautiful
      Clouds o' gold and white and blue!—
Month a man kin railly love—
June, you know, I'm talkin' of!

VIII

March ain't never nothin' new!—
Aprile's altogether too
  Brash fer me! and May—I jes'
  'Bominate its promises,—
Little hints o' sunshine and
Green around the timber-land—
  A few blossoms, and a few
  Chip-birds, and a sprout er two,—
  Drap asleep, and it turns in
  'Fore daylight and *snows* ag'in!—
But when *June* comes—Clear my th'oat
  With wild honey!—Rench my hair

In the dew! and hold my coat!
    Whoop out loud! and th'ow my hat!—
June wants me, and I'm to spare!
Spread them shadders anywhere,
I'll git down and waller there,
    And obleeged to you at that!

THE LAW OF THE PERVERSE

WHERE did the custom come from, any-
      way—
  Sending the boys to "play," at dinner-time,
When we have company? What is there, pray,
    About the starched, unmalleable *guest*
    That, in the host's most genial interest,
Finds *him* first favor on Thanksgiving Day
  Beside the steaming turkey, with its wings
  Akimbo over all the savory things
  It has been stuffed with, yet may never thus
  Make one poor boy's face glad and glorious!

Fancy the exiled boy in the back yard,
  Ahungered so, that any kind of grub
Were welcome, yet with face set stern and hard,
  Hearing the feasters' mirth and mild hubbub,
  And wanting to kill something with a club!—
  Intuitively arguing the unjust
  Distinction, as he naturally must,—
  The guest with all the opportunity—
  The boy with all the appetite! Ah, me!

So is it that, when I, a luckless guest,
  Am thus arraigned at banquet, I sit grim
And sullen, eating nothing with a zest,—
With smirking features, yet a soul distressed,
  Missing the banished boy and envying him—
Ay, longing for a spatter on my vest
    From his deflecting spoon, and yearning for
    The wild swoop of his lips insatiate, or
    His ever-ravenous, marauding eye
    Fore-eating everything, from soup to pie!

OUT OF NAZARETH

"HE shall sleep unscathed of thieves
    Who loves Allah and believes."
Thus heard one who shared the tent,
In the far-off Orient,
Of the Bedouin ben Ahrzz—
Nobler never loved the stars
Through the palm-leaves nigh the dim
Dawn his courser neighed to him!

He said: "Let the sands be swarmed
    With such thieves as I, and thou
Shalt at morning rise, unharmed,
    Light as eyelash to the brow
Of thy camel, amber-eyed,
Ever munching either side,
Striding still, with nestled knees,
Through the midnight's oases.

"Who can rob thee an thou hast
More than this that thou hast cast
At my feet—this dust of gold?
Simply this and that, all told!
Hast thou not a treasure of
Such a thing as men call love?

"Can the dusky band I lead
Rob thee of thy daily need
Of a whiter soul, or steal
What thy lordly prayers reveal?
Who could be enriched of thee
By such hoard of poverty
As thy niggard hand pretends
To dole me—thy worst of friends?
Therefore shouldst thou pause to bless
One indeed who blesses thee:
Robbing thee, I dispossess
But myself.—Pray thou for me!"

"He shall sleep unscathed of thieves
Who loves Allah and believes."

TIME

I

THE ticking—ticking—ticking of the clock!—
   That vexed me so last night!—"For though
      Time keeps
  Such drowsy watch," I moaned, "he never sleeps,
But only nods above the world to mock
Its restless occupant, then rudely rock
  It as the cradle of a babe that weeps!"
  I seemed to see the seconds piled in heaps
Like sand about me; and at every shock
  O' the bell, the pilèd sands were swirled away
As by a desert-storm that swept the earth
  Stark as a granary floor, whereon the gray
And mist-bedrizzled moon amidst the dearth
  Came crawling, like a sickly child, to lay
  Its pale face next mine own and weep for day.

II

Wait for the morning! Ah! we wait indeed
  For daylight, we who toss about through stress
  Of vacant-armed desires and emptiness
Of all the warm, warm touches that we need,

And the warm kisses upon which we feed
  Our famished lips in fancy! May God bless
  The starved lips of us with but one caress
Warm as the yearning blood our poor hearts bleed!
. . . A wild prayer!—bite thy pillow, praying so—
  Toss this side, and whirl that, and moan for
     dawn;
Let the clock's seconds dribble out their woe
And Time be drained of sorrow! Long ago
  We heard the crowing cock, with answer drawn
  As hoarsely sad at throat as sobs. . . . Pray on!

IKE WALTON'S PRAYER

I CRAVE, dear Lord,
  No boundless hoard
 Of gold and gear,
   Nor jewels fine,
   Nor lands, nor kine,
Nor treasure-heaps of anything.—
   Let but a little hut be mine
  Where at the hearthstone I may hear
    The cricket sing,
    And have the shine
  Of one glad woman's eyes to make,
  For my poor sake,
    Our simple home a place divine;—
Just the wee cot—the cricket's chirr—
Love, and the smiling face of her.

   I pray not for
   Great riches, nor
  For vast estates and castle halls,—
  Give me to hear the bare footfalls
    Of children o'er
    An oaken floor
  New-rinsed with sunshine, or bespread

With but the tiny coverlet
And pillow for the baby's head;
And, pray Thou, may
The door stand open and the day
 Send ever in a gentle breeze,
  With fragrance from the locust trees,
   And drowsy moan of doves, and blur
Of robin-chirps, and drone of bees,
  With after-hushes of the stir
Of intermingling sounds, and then
  The goodwife and the smile of her
Filling the silences again—
   The cricket's call
    And the wee cot,
   Dear Lord of all,
    Deny me not!

 I pray not that
 Men tremble at
 My power of place
  And lordly sway,—
I only pray for simple grace
To look my neighbor in the face
 Full honestly from day to day—
Yield me his horny palm to hold,
  And I'll not pray
   For gold;—
The tanned face, garlanded with mirth,
It hath the kingliest smile on earth;
The swart brow, diamonded with sweat,

Hath never need of coronet.
           'And so I reach,
                Dear Lord, to Thee,
           'And do beseech
                Thou givest me
The wee cot, and the cricket's chirr,
Love, and the glad sweet face of her!

THE WAY IT WUZ

LAS' July—and, I persume,
    'Bout as hot
As the old Gran'-jury room
    Whare they sot!—
Fight 'twixt Mike and Dock McGreff. . . .
'Pears to me jes' like as ef
    I'd a-dremp' the whole blame thing—
        Allus ha'nts me roun' the gizzard
    When they's nightmares on the wing
        And a feller's blood's jes' friz!
    Seed the row from A to Izzard—
    'Cause I wuz a-standin' as clos't to 'em
        As me and you is!

Tell you the way it wuz—
    And I don't *want* to see,
Like *some* fellers does,
    When they's goern to be
Any kind o' fuss—
On'y makes a rumpus wuss
    Fer to *interfere*
        When theyr dander's riz—
    Might as lif to *cheer!*
But I wuz a-standin' as clos't to 'em
        As me and you is!

I wuz kind o' strayin'
  Past the blame saloon—
Heerd some fiddler playin'
  That old "Hee-cup tune!"
I'd *stopped*-like, you know,
Fer a minit er so,
  And wuz jes' about
Settin' down, when—*Jeemses-whizz!*—
  Whole durn winder-sash fell out!
And thare laid Dock McGreff, and Mike
A-straddlin' him, all bloody-like,
  And both a-gittin' down to biz!—
And I wuz a-standin' as clos't to 'em
  As me and you is!

I wuz the on'y man aroun'—
  (Durn old-fogey town!
   'Peared more like, to me,
   Sund'y than *Saturd'y!*)
  Dog come 'crost the road
   And tuk a smell
    And putt right back:
  Mishler driv by 'ith a load
   O' cantalo'pes he couldn't sell—
    Too mad, 'i jack!
  To even ast
  What wuz up, as he went past!
Weather most outrageous hot!—
  Fairly hear it sizz

Roun' Dock and Mike—tel Dock he shot,—
   And Mike he slacked that grip o' his
   And fell, all spraddled out. Dock riz
 'Bout half up, a-spittin' red,
 And shuck his head. . . .
And I wuz a-standin' as clos't to 'em
   As me and you is!

And Dock he says,
  A-whisperin'-like,—
   "It hain't no use
  A-tryin'!—Mike
   He's jes' ripped my daylights loose!—
Git that blame-don fiddler to
Let up, and come out here—You
Got some burryin' to do,—
  Mike makes *one,* and, I expects,
'Bout ten seconds, I'll make *two!*"
  And he drapped back, whare he'd riz,
'Crost Mike's body, black and blue,
  Like a great big letter X!—
And I wuz a-standin' as clos't to 'em
  As me and you is!

CURLY LOCKS

CURLY Locks! Curly Locks! wilt thou be mine?
Thou shalt not wash the dishes, nor yet feed
the swine,—
But sit on a cushion and sew a fine seam,
And feast upon strawberries, sugar and cream.

Curly Locks! Curly Locks! wilt thou be mine?
The throb of my heart is in every line,
And the pulse of a passion as airy and glad
In its musical beat as the little Prince had!

Thou shalt not wash the dishes, nor yet feed the
swine!—
O I'll dapple thy hands with these kisses of mine
Till the pink of the nail of each finger shall be
As a little pet blush in full blossom for me.

But sit on a cushion and sew a fine seam,
And thou shalt have fabric as fair as a dream,—
The red of my veins, and the white of my love,
And the gold of my joy for the braiding thereof.

And feast upon strawberries, sugar and cream
From a service of silver, with jewels agleam,—
At thy feet will I bide, at thy beck will I rise,
And twinkle my soul in the night of thine eyes!

Curly Locks! Curly Locks! wilt thou be mine?
Thou shalt not wash the dishes, nor yet feed the
swine,—
But sit on a cushion and sew a fine seam,
And feast upon strawberries, sugar and cream.